COOK FOR A DAY,
EAT FOR A MONTH

FROZEN ASSETS
READERS' FAVORITES

deborah taylor-hough

CHAMPION PRESS LTD.

Milwaukee, Wisconsin

Other books by Deborah Taylor-Hough

Frozen Assets: how to cook for a day and eat for a month
(ISBN 1-891400-61-4)

*Frozen Assets Lite & Easy: how to cook for a day and eat for a
month* (ISBN 1-891400-28-2)

Mix and Match Recipes: creative recipes for busy kitchens
(ISBN 1-891400-07-X)

*A Simple Choice: a practical guide for saving your time, money
and sanity* (ISBN 1-891400-49-5)

To order visit your favorite bookseller or order online at
www.championpress.com

A Special Thanks...

We would like to send a big thank you to all of the contributors and recipe winners featured in this book. Between their new recipes and favorites from Deborah's first two books, *Frozen Assets: how to cook for a day and eat for a month* and *Frozen Assets Lite & Easy: how to cook for a day and eat for a month*, we are very pleased to bring you this volume of favorites for your freezer.

contributors and recipe winners

SARA PATTOW	ELIZABETH BISHOP
KATHY GULAN	PENNY STONE
LEANNE ELY	BROOK NOEL
WENDY LOUISE	DEENA JACOBS
J.B. BRYANT	KIM ADAMS
CAROL R. GEHRINGER	MARY ANN KLOTZ
LISA MARIE LEONARD	DAWN POPE
JESSICA D. CARTER	MICHELE BARNES
JENNIFER L. DAWSON	MELANIE LABARDINI
DONA B WUNSCHEL	BEVERLY CARROLL
CHRISTINA RENEE HIGGINS	KIMBERLY MIELOCH
DARLENE FEIEREISEN	ERIN LUDIN
JOAN EGAN	ANNE PEIFFER
SHIRLEY YVONNE DE VARENNES	

Contents

CHAPTER ONE

Cooking for the Freezer

AN INTRODUCTION TO ONCE-A-MONTH-COOKING

What if I told you I had a way for you to gain an extra hour each day . . . or seven hours per week . . . or nearly thirty hours per month? Would you start wondering if I'd fallen out of the crib onto my head a few too many times as a baby? Well, this deal is for real. I have a commodity to offer that's more valuable than gold . . . or land . . . or diamonds. That precious gem I can offer you is called: Time!

Wouldn't you love to free up quantities of time each and every day? Time that could be spent sitting down with your spouse on the couch, or actually putting your feet up after work for a few undisturbed moments? Wouldn't your children relish curling up in a parent's lap for a cuddle and a chapter from the family's latest read-aloud book before dinner?

And wouldn't you really love having an easy answer to that perennial question, "What's for dinner?"

What's for dinner tonight could be as simple as something you whip together in fifteen to twenty minutes: Salisbury steak, homemade fish chowder, Aunt Emily's favorite lasagna, roast turkey with all the fixings, marinated chicken breasts or whatever else your family enjoys eating. And you won't spend an hour or two slaving over a hot stove every night to achieve these culinary miracles. They might just require the minor effort of throwing a baking dish into the oven and forgetting about it for an hour; or stirring something over a stovetop burner just until it's heated through. Make a salad, slice some French bread, fresh from the corner bakery and voila', you have a dinner that would make Martha proud!

Crisis Meal Planning

If your home is anything like mine, you've probably found that five o'clock each evening is one of the most hectic times of the day. Mom and dad are just finishing up a long day of work at home or at the office. The kids are hungry and tired after a full day of school and afternoon sports. It's time to fix supper or at least we should be getting dinner started if we want to eat a meal before midnight! But what's for dinner tonight? Well, your guess is probably as good as mine . . . and it seems like more often than not, nobody knows! So the whole family hops in the car and heads through the local drive-thru for the third time in a week.

Someone I know once called this "crisis" meal planning. Each night's dinner is the latest in a string of mealtime crisis-management decisions. Everyone's tired. The kids are hungry. The whining is starting in earnest. What's a parent to do?

"What will we have to eat? Um . . . well . . . I just heard that Fred's Diner is having a sale on cheeseburgers this week. Let's go! Everyone in the car!"

Rather than planning ahead to prevent panic and poor nutritional choices, many families coast through their days without giving a thought to dinner and then discover they've crashed headlong into that nightly mealtime crisis once again.

Cooking ahead for the freezer can be the answer to this all-too-frequent mealtime dilemma. The process of cooking an entire month's worth of meals, in one day, is an efficient and cost-saving alternative for many families, but spending eight hours in the kitchen is daunting for some who would like to try this method. The mini-session is the perfect answer for these people.

Whether you choose to triple recipes during your regular meal preparations, cook a full month of meals at a time or simply choose a mini-session or two, you'll find this method will save not only your time, but also your money and sanity. No more "crisis" meal planning; you'll have dinner on the table regularly with little-more fuss than heating a thawed freezer meal and adding a quick salad or side dish.

But Isn't it a Leftover?

Many people worry that eating meals from the freezer will be like having leftovers every night. But it's not. You won't be eating something that's been cooked completely, and then reheated, and then reheated again. You're eating food that has either been frozen before cooking (so it's cooked up fresh on serving day) or you're eating food that's been cooked just until barely done, frozen and then reheated just enough to serve. If food is cooked and stored properly, frozen dinners can be as tasty as fresh.

Financial Freedom

I first started cooking ahead for the time-saving benefits. It helped bring our family together again around the table. But I was quickly surprised by another benefit that I didn't foresee. Our grocery bill went down by almost $400 per month! I couldn't believe it! Some of the money we saved was due to the fact that we had been eating out quite frequently, quickly running down to the corner for .59 cent tacos because I hadn't had time to cook dinner. Now we always have time for dinner at home—we eat out when we want to, not because we feel we have to. Going out to eat has become a special treat rather than an expensive and unhealthy way of life.

By cooking ahead, I was able to begin buying commonly-used items in bulk. I was also planning my menus ahead of time. Just the planning ahead and bulk buying saved a lot of money. But $400 per month? Wow! And that was the average I was shaving off our grocery bill each month! Sometimes we saved even more than that. This method also eliminated waste, and because I don't go to the store nearly as often as I used to, it also cuts down on those expensive impulse buys at the market.

I now take full advantage of sales at the grocery store, planning menus around their weekly specials. If ground beef is on sale, I'll buy a large amount and then prepare a quantity of ground beef recipes to put in the freezer. Rather than doing a full month of cooking, I'll do what I refer to as a ground beef mini-session. This involves preparing a week or two of ground beef recipes to be interspersed with the chicken or tofu recipes I prepared during earlier chicken and tofu mini-sessions. With a combination of these mini-sessions I can stash away "Frozen Assets" for the next two or three months. But in addition to the time and money-saving benefits, I discovered many other perks.

Not only did cooking ahead solve the meal planning and time issues, it also provided me with a way to help our family's financial situation. Money was quite tight and I had been thinking of getting a part-time job to help make ends meet. I found cutting back a bit on what I was spending on groceries could mean the difference between remaining at home with my children or going back to work. I wouldn't cut back on the amount of food we ate, so we still ate well, but by being conscientious about meal planning and buying on sale, we shaved sizeable amounts off our monthly food budget. Saving $400 per month from our approximately $700 per month grocery budget became "my part time job". Over the course of five years, I spent $24,000 less on groceries!

Hospitality

Frozen meals can be used for hospitality and outreach. Dinner parties are a breeze. If we want to spontaneously invite people over after church, it's not a difficult ordeal. I know I have things in the freezer that I can quickly and easily heat and serve. You can have meals available for the sick or for people in need. Bringing a couple of frozen meals to a new mother or a grieving family can bring a touch of sanity to an otherwise stressful time of life. I don't even have to think about it or plan for it. I just grab something from the freezer and go.

Following the premature birth of our first child, a group of friends from church filled our freezer with over two weeks of frozen meals. Between frequent visits to the hospital nursery and the normal stresses of starting a new family, those meals in the freezer were a lifesaver. During a later pregnancy, I wound up on bed rest for nearly four weeks. Once again, the ladies from church came to our aid with frozen dinners. One woman overwhelmed me when she showed up at my door laden with several shopping bags full of ready-to-cook frozen dinners—all from her personal stock of freezer meals.

The meals brought after my daughter's premature birth were my introduction to the concept of frozen meals. Since then, I've applied this method to our regular family menus and have saved substantial time, effort and money in the process. Some cookbooks refer to this as investment cooking, once-a-month cooking, bulk-cooking or cooking ahead. I call my method "Frozen Assets", since dinner in the freezer can be like money in the bank.

Whether you're a stay-at-home mom creatively trying to make ends meet, a working parent searching for more hours in your hectic day, a single person looking for ideas for preparing home cooked meals without leftovers, someone interested in the outreach opportunities frozen meals can provide, or anyone who needs to save money or find a few more hours in their day, "Frozen Assets" could be your answer.

No More Kitchen Slavery

During those rare times when I run out of my "Frozen Assets" stash, it's a rude awakening to see just how "daily" food preparation is in a busy home. As I often say when doing my workshops—"I like cooking—I just don't like it every day!" Between all the planning and actual preparation for each meal, it can begin to seem like the kitchen is a harsh taskmaster, not even allowing time off for good behavior. The "daily-ness" of cooking wears us down quickly. By having meals ready to go in the freezer, I find that the joy of cooking has been restored for me. When I do decide to cook a special meal, it's a joy again and not just another chore to be accomplished as quickly as possible. I also have more time and energy for "fun cooking"— baking cookies with my children or making fresh, hot gingerbread on a cold-winter evening.

Restoring the Family Dinner Hour

Recently, there was a story in my local newspaper about the disappearance of the family dinner hour. With more and more double-income families and children involved in numerous after school and sports activities, the family dinner hour has gone the way of the dinosaur.

Yet my family sits down together for dinner at least five times each week. How often do you sit down, as a family, at the table for a leisurely meal? Four times a week? Twice? Once? I'm not super woman; I'm simply someone who discovered a way to reap the benefits of advanced planning and preparation. Now these benefits can be yours. I'll show you how to make it happen, step-by-step. If you'd like to restore this time-honored tradition in your home, cooking for the freezer can be the solution. So what are you waiting for? Let's get started. I recommend that people begin this process gradually. If the idea of a full month of cooking sounds overwhelming, start small. If two weeks sounds more do-able, try cooking ahead for two weeks. Or try one week.

But if cooking for even a week at a time sounds like more than you can fathom, try this: In the course of your normal cooking, triple your recipes. If you're preparing lasagna, make three—one for eating tonight and two for the freezer. Tomorrow night do the same thing with a different recipe. After one week of tripling your regular meals and freezing two, you'll have two weeks of meals with almost no extra effort. It's really not much harder to prepare three lasagnas than it is to prepare one. Or make a large pot of spaghetti sauce rather than a single family serving and freeze the extras in meal-size servings.

If you think cooking ahead is a process you'd like to try, but you're unsure of the amount of work involved, ease into it. Start out by doubling and tripling recipes as you go through your week. Maybe do a ground beef mini-session next time there's a sale at the grocery store. What you will find is that you will start saving time, you'll start saving money, and you won't be doing this in an overwhelming or difficult manner. Each time you pull one of those meals out of the freezer you'll be pleased.

Small Freezer Syndrome

Many people tell me they only have a small fridge-top freezer so they don't think they can do a full month of meals. That was my excuse for not trying this method at first but I've found, with practice, I can pack a full thirty meals in my refrigerator-freezer. The last time I did a big cooking day, I counted forty-four meals in my small freezer. I have a separate freezer now, but I usually use it for stocking things like ice cream or bread I find on sale at the bakery thrift store. I keep my prepared meals in the small kitchen freezer where they're easily accessible.

Probably the most practical suggestion for people with a small freezer is to use zip-top freezer bags. These bags take up a lot less room than bulkier storage containers such as plastic boxes or aluminum pans. Freezer bags that are already "doubled" are now available for extra durability.

Clear out all non-essentials on cooking day if you only have a small freezer. When I only had my refrigerator-freezer, I would wait until mid-month to stock up on extras like ice cream or frozen bread. I used this cooking technique for over three years with only a small fridge-top freezer, so it can be done. It just takes careful planning and packing.

To save space, you can also prepare sauces to serve over pasta or rice, but don't make the pasta or rice ahead of time. Cook the pasta or rice at serving time. Usually the sauce is the time-consuming part of fixing dinner, so by fixing the pasta or rice fresh, it not only tastes better but allows you to use your freezer space more efficiently.

Storage Tip

Lay freezer bags flat and then stand them on end after they're frozen solid. Your freezer shelf will look like it contains LP record albums filled with frozen food and you won't experience a landslide of frozen packages when you open the freezer door.

Freezer Containers

I want to assure you that you don't need to hold a party and buy expensive plastic boxes. Any food-grade plastic will work. The inexpensive plastic boxes at the grocery store function just fine, but make sure you purchase storage items with tight fitting, air-tight lids. If you want to invest money in the higher quality plastic boxes, by all means feel free. You definitely get what you pay for. And the fancy, expensive home-party boxes usually last for many years and come with replacement guarantees. I just want to assure people that you don't *have* to stock your freezer shelves with designer containers. The only plastic freezer containers I own are the inexpensive ones from the grocery store and they have served me well for many years.

FOOD CONTAINERS: You can freeze food items in clean, plastic margarine containers if that's all you have, but the seal isn't really air-tight so don't freeze these items for longer than two weeks or the quality of the food will suffer. It's important to remember that margarine containers are safe for freezing good (they are made of food grade plastic), but don't reheat your meal in them. They're not microwave-able, and they can seep harmful chemicals into your family's food. Be sure that a plastic container is labeled "microwave safe" before using it to reheat food.

If you have a choice between round or rectangular freezer containers, choose rectangular. These utilize space more efficiently, taking up less room in the freezer.

ALUMINUM FOIL PANS: You can also use disposable aluminum foil pans purchased at the grocery store. These can often be reused several times before needing to be recycled or disposed. Disposable pans are ideal if you're making meals to use to give to others; the recipient doesn't need to worry about returning your pan or casserole dish. If clean up is a huge time-consumer, disposable pans can be easily thrown away, making cleanup painless.

I've built up a good supply of freezer containers by stocking up on bake ware and other freeze-able containers at garage sales and thrift stores. Glass bake ware works fine. When wrapping pans for the freezer, be sure to use good quality heavy-duty freezer foil.

FREEZER BAGS: I personally use zip-top freezer bags for most of my food storage needs. Not only do they take up less space than boxes, the bags are inexpensive and easy to use. It's important to buy top quality freezer bags—this isn't the place to cut back, money-wise. There's nothing worse for a "freezer-meal-cook" than to have your entire batch of frozen meals ruined by poor wrapping or freezer bags breaking. I recommend double-bagging anything that has a soupy consistency so you don't end up with a watery mess at the bottom of your refrigerator after the meal thaws. Sometimes bags can develop small holes or the zip-top can open slightly.

FOIL: You can also make your own freezer pans by lining a casserole dish with foil. Put the food in on top of the foil, freeze the meal until it's solid, and then remove the foil and food from the dish. Finish wrapping the frozen meal and put it back into the freezer. When it's time to serve the meal, simply place the foil-wrapped meal back into the original dish that was used to freeze and mold it. Thaw and reheat in the original dish. This method keeps your pans available for other uses during the month.

Labeling Your Freezer Meals

You want to make sure you label everything carefully and accurately. When food is frozen, many meals look the same. One tomato-based meal will look like a dozen other tomato-based meals. You don't want to play "Guess the Freezer Meal" when you're trying to get your family's dinner on the table each night.

MARKER LABELING: I recommend using Sharpie™ brand permanent markers for labeling. You can actually write directly on the freezer bags and even on the aluminum foil. I want to emphasize: Don't use any other brand of permanent marker to write on your freezer bags or foil. There are other brands of permanent markers, but Sharpie™ is the only one I've found that won't wipe off. I previously worked in a medical lab and we were required to carry a Sharpie™ with us at all times. The lab managers wouldn't let us use any other brand of marker. We wrote on beakers, test tubes, petri dishes

A Freezer Inventory

There is nothing worse than opening your freezer to find unidentifiable frozen masses. Careful labeling of your meals will avoid this problem. A freezer inventory is another valuable tool. Simply write down each recipe you have in your freezer in the left hand column. Next to the name, write the quantity you have prepared. Each time you remove a freezer meal, mark the quantity down by one. I have provided a worksheet you can use in Section Five.

and slides, and then those items went through assorted chemical baths. The labels written with Sharpies™ wouldn't come off. You don't want to lose your labels so it's important to use the best labeler available.

LABELING WITH INDEX CARDS: Another way of labeling items stored in freezer bags is to double bag the food and slip a 3"x5" file card with the instructions between the freezer bags. The outer bag and the label can both be reused indefinitely with this method. This can be handy if you prepare the same meals often when cooking for the freezer. You can prepare half a dozen labels ahead of time and not have to spend that time and effort with each cooking experience. Also, make sure to include your reheating instructions on each label. This way you can prep the meal quickly and easily without having to dig through a recipe box, or cookbook, at serving time.

What to Freeze, What Not to Freeze

When I started cooking for the freezer, I was amazed to find more things freeze well than don't. I thought there must be some special criteria for deciphering whether or not a meal would freeze well. But almost anything can be frozen. Take a walk down your grocery store's frozen food aisle sometime and just notice the wide variety of items that can be frozen ahead.

Foods that freeze well:

Baked goods (most)
Beans (dry), cooked
Burgers
Breakfast burritos
Breakfast casseroles
Brownies
Cakes
Calzones
Casseroles
Cookies
Egg rolls
Enchiladas
French toast
Fruit sauces
Fudge

Grains, cooked (rice, barley, bulgur, couscous)
Hamburger patties, uncooked
Quiche
Quick breads
Lasagna
Main dishes
Manicotti
Marinated meats
Mashed potatoes
Meatballs
Meatloaf
Meat pies
Meats for roasting (beef, chicken lamb, pork)
Muffins

Pancakes
Pies
Pot pies
Poultry
Sandwiches
Sauces
Sloppy Joes

Soups
Stuffed shells
Taco/burrito fillings
Tofu
Turkey
TVP (texturized vegetable protein)
Waffles

Things that don't freeze well tend to be egg-based sauces, milk or cream-based sauces (they separate but can be recombined after thawing), instant rice, raw salad ingredients, stuffed poultry, dishes with dried toppings, baked fruit pies, mayonnaise (unless it's mixed in and used as part of a sauce), cottage cheese, raw clams, hard cooked eggs and fried foods.

Cooking for Your Specific Diet

One of the most frequently asked questions I hear about this method of cooking is, "What about vegetarians? How can vegetarians apply this to how they eat?" Freezer cooking for vegetarian eating really isn't a problem. When you're making a meal, take out a sample serving, freeze it, reheat it and see how it turns out. If it turns out well, then you have a successful freezer meal to add to your "Frozen Assets" repertoire. I recommend this single-serving trial process for any meal you're not sure will freeze well. Tofu, TVP (texturized vegetable protein) and cooked dry beans all freeze well. Many people say they actually prefer the texture of pre-frozen tofu; it dries out a bit and becomes a little firmer. Also, many of the recipes in this book can be prepared without meat; just leave out the meat altogether or switch the meat item with your favorite meat substitute.

All of us eat differently. Each family has different meal preferences. I don't necessarily recommend using either of my books on freezer cooking as your freezer meal Bible. Don't feel you can only use the recipes in my books and never venture off to use your own recipes. Try several of the meal plans in these books to get started and get a feel for how the process works, but ultimately I hope readers will take these methods and apply them to their own recipes and ways of eating.

Trial and Error

At times this style of cooking can be a bit of a trial and error process. We all make occasional mistakes but we learn from them and move on. I'll share with you some of the ptifalls I recommend watching for during meal preparation and planning. Feel free to learn from my experiences.

Be sure to keep track of which meals you've used and which ones are still in the freezer. A few times I've forgotten to keep an accurate record and at the end of the month, found myself staring at four or five bags of spaghetti sauce with nothing else in the freezer for our last week of the month. My family and I didn't want to eat a full week of spaghetti sauce but that was all that was left. If you don't keep track, you may end up with a large amount of one type of meal at the end of your month. By planning ahead and marking off the meals as you use them, you can space your meals for more of an assortment week by week. I recommend using a magnetic dry-erase board that can hang on the side of your refrigerator. Simply write down what you have put in your freezer (and when) and then cross it off once used. This makes it easy to get a quick grasp on what you have and what you need as you do your menu planning.

I've also found that noodles can completely disappear from frozen soups. If you cook noodles all the way until they're soft before freezing, when you take your soup out of the freezer, thaw it and reheat it, you'll find you don't have any noodles left. If you want noodles in your soup, wait until you're reheating the soup at serving time to throw in the noodles. The noodles will cook while the soup is reheating. Or, toss the raw noodles into the freezer bag with the soup just before placing the bag into the freezer.

Another tip to remember is: Moderation in all things. I tend to stock up on meats and food items when they go on sale. One time a friend called to let me know a local store was having a sale on ground turkey for forty pounds for $12. I ran down to the store and bought forty pounds of ground turkey. I was so proud of myself! $12? That's at least forty meals worth of meat for a mere pittance. But six months later we still had ground turkey in the freezer that we were working our way through. My family likes ground turkey, but I discovered they didn't like forty pounds worth. If I had purchased ten pounds, I still would've made a wonderful bargain and my family would've been much happier.

I have also created a message board for those "Frozen Asset Cooks" who want to share their tips and recipes, and to learn more. For further information, go to: http://hometown.aol.com/oamcloop/index.html or check out the cooking resources on the following page.

Wishing you the best,

Deborah Taylor-Hough

COOKING RESOURCES

All Recipes - Although not devoted just to cooking for the freezer, you can view many wonderful recipes, which are adaptable to this cooking method, at www.allrecipes.com

Busy Cooks - A great site for any busy cook looking for great recipes and time-saving ideas.

The Rush Hour Cook - A fun site that will have you laughing while you're cooking, with down-to-earth-practical fare that can be prepared by the self-proclaimed "Queen of Inept Cooking."

The Open Directory Project - You'll find a whole slew of freezer-friendly sites inside Google's directory project. Simply go to www.google.com and click on *DIRECTORY*. Then choose *HOME*. Select *FOOD* from your next choices and you'll see the section devoted to freezer fans.

CHAPTER TWO

Creating A 30-Day Meal Plan

Remember, you don't have to do a full month of meals at once. You can choose to do mini-sessions and stock up gradually, or you can do a week or two at a time. In Chapter Nine, I have provided plans of all types to get you started. I know some of you will still want to go visit uncharted territory and create your own plan... so here are the steps.

STEP ONE

Choose ten to fifteen recipes

First, choose ten to fifteen different recipes, depending upon how often your family is willing to eat the same thing over the course of a month. Usually I can get away with feeding my family the same thing three times during a month. So for my family's tastes and preferences, I can prepare ten different recipes, tripling each one for a month's worth of thirty meals. If your family only wants to eat the same thing twice a month, then you would need to choose fifteen different recipes. If your family only wants to eat things once a month, you have a lot more work to do because you won't be doubling or tripling your recipes. Thirty completely different recipes can be done; it's just a good deal harder and more time-consuming. The fewer individual recipes you use the better, as far as time, energy and monetary expenditures, when doing this type of cooking.

STEP TWO

Plan your meals for the month

I try to make sure I spread the recipes apart during the month. My family might not be willing to eat the same meal three days in a row, but they're more than happy to eat the same meal if it's spread a week and a half apart. What I do to ensure I've spaced meals properly is to take a blank calendar page and fill it out ahead of time. First, I'll figure out what we're going to eat. I'll try to vary things. We'll want to have a certain number of chicken, ground beef, and vegetarian meals, so I try to divide them up over the

> ### A Sticky Menu Plan
>
> Another easy way to plan your 30 day-meal plan is to use sticky notes. Write down individual recipes you would like to try on sticky notes. Use a large calendar page to stick each note to a date and then rearrange them until you have a plan you are satisfied with.

course of the month. By planning ahead, I can see where I'm going with my monthly meal plan. Otherwise, I might find that I've forgotten to make a variety of meals for the month, maybe forgetting to make chicken recipes, or making too many ground beef meals.

Planning ahead really helps when you're making out your monthly menus. You can plan your recipes around what's on sale at the grocery store the week you'll be cooking. I also look through my freezer, refrigerator and cupboards to see what I already have on hand to use in my current meal plan.

STEP THREE

Make your shopping list

After you decide what you're going to make, go through your recipes, writing down every single ingredient and the exact amounts that you'll need. Go through your cupboards, refrigerator and freezer, checking off all ingredients you already have on hand, making certain you have the full amount needed. If you need four (16 ounce) cans of tomato sauce, you need to make sure that you actually

The Major Master Plan
You can save time by creating a master plan for your household. Walk through your house recording everything that needs to be replenished from toiletries to light bulbs. Use this as your monthly starting point. We have included a master plan in Section Three to get you started.

have that total amount in ounces. If you only have two (8 ounce) cans of sauce, you'll need to make a note about how many ounces of tomato sauce you still need to purchase.

After you've gone through all your supplies and your cupboards, the items still remaining on your list of ingredients will be your actual shopping list.

STEP FOUR

Gather freezer containers

You'll want to figure out what type of freezer containers you'll be needing and how many. You'll add these items to your shopping list as well. Take into account aluminum foil, disposable pans, plastic containers, plastic wrap, freezer bags (assorted sizes), labels, marking pens, etc.

STEP FIVE

Prepare your refrigerator & freezer

The most important thing to do before you head to the grocery store is to thoroughly clean out your refrigerator and freezer. You'll need to make room for all the food that you'll be bringing home from the market. It won't be in the refrigerator very long because you'll be adding it into prepared meals to store in the freezer, but you don't want to find yourself staring at a full refrigerator while you're trying to unload multiple bags of groceries filled with perishable food items.

If possible, you'll also want to turn the thermostat setting on your freezer to -10 degrees 24 hours before adding large amounts of newly prepared food to your freezer on your cooking day.

STEP SIX

Put away perishables first

After you're done shopping, put away all of your perishables but leave out on the counter, your canned goods and anything that doesn't need to be refrigerated overnight. Putting canned goods away just to take them out again in the morning is definitely an inefficient way to use your time and energy at this point. Trust me! Any steps saved on that big cooking day will be appreciated.

Hang Your Recipes

Consider placing your recipes in a plastic protector so they aren't subject to splatters and spills. Taping the page protectors in a row along your cabinet at eye level will make preparation easier.

STEP SEVEN

Separate your recipes

Separate your recipes according to main ingredients or main protein: chicken, ground beef, ham, dried beans, etc. Plan on preparing your recipes in groups, according to their main ingredients. Essentially what you're doing on a big cooking day is a series of mini-sessions. For example do all the chicken recipes at one time, then all the ground beef recipes, then all your dry bean recipes.

STEP EIGHT

Prepare ahead

Assemble all necessary utensils ahead of time: pots, pans, measuring cups, measuring spoons, stirring spoons, wire whisks, appliances, bake ware, freezer containers, etc. It's a good idea to have two complete sets of measuring spoons and measuring cups—one for dry ingredients, the other for wet.

Look through your recipes and break them down into individual steps. You'll want to do similar steps together: brown all the ground beef at once, chop all the vegetables, prepare and de-bone all the chicken, cook all the beans. You don't want to have four or five little sessions of browning ground beef as you go through your recipes; do it all together at one time. I find doing many of these things the night before the "big cooking day" is very helpful. In an hour and a half, the night before, I can quickly prepare spaghetti sauce, brown the ground beef, cook the chicken, chop the onions and celery, and grate any cheeses. This saves a great deal of time and effort for the next day.

Plan on preparing your most complicated recipes first thing in the day while you're still fresh. If you have anything that's time-consuming or requires a lot of thought or quick movement, get it done before you move on to easier recipes.

STEP NINE

Take care of yourself

Cooking for a month can be a tiring proposition. It's a long day and it's a lot of work, but it doesn't have to be unbearable if you take simple steps to care for yourself.

Remember to think about your comfort and energy level as you go through the day. Get a good night's sleep the night before. Dress comfortably. Wear supportive shoes. This isn't the day to cook barefoot. If you have nurse's shoes, or you've ever worked as a waitress and still have

> ### Defining a Day
>
> If doing this whole process in a single day sounds too overwhelming, spread it out over several. Shop one day. Do basic prep on another day. Prepare your meals on yet another day.

the shoes, that type of footwear is ideal for a long day of standing on your feet Some people even wear hiking boots on cooking day. Wear the most supportive shoes you have in the house. Tie back long hair or wear a hairnet. Put on an apron, even if you don't usually wear one. If you're ever going to make a big mess in the kitchen, this will be the day.

Make it fun: play upbeat music, sing, dance and remember to smile.

Be sure to eat breakfast in the morning. Remember to stop for lunch (and actually sit down while you eat it!). I find I can get so involved with the cooking process, I forget to eat all day. Take frequent mini-breaks. Pull up a high stool next to the counter so you can sit down often. Do as much meal preparation as possible sitting at the kitchen table or counter.

STEP TEN

Keep it clean

Fill a sink with hot, soapy water so you can wash your pots and pans and measuring utensils as you go. Wash your hands frequently, especially after handling raw meats. Tuck a kitchen towel into the waistband of your apron so it's handy for quickly mopping up messes and spills.

STEP ELEVEN

Prevent overcooking

To prevent overcooking, or that warmed-over taste, slightly undercook foods to be reheated after freezing. For example, if you're preparing a lasagna requiring a one hour baking time, cut the time down to 50 minutes, freeze the lasagna at that point, and then the meal will complete the last ten minutes of cooking during the reheating process. If you cook things all the way and then freeze and reheat, you'll get into the realm of feeling you're eating leftovers. Overcooked food will start tasting "warmed up" rather than fresh.

STEP TWELVE

Package, label & freeze your food

Pack food in quantities to be used for family-sized meals. You may also want to consider packing single-serving sizes for quick lunches. I have a friend whose husband travels three to five days a week. She prepares individual lasagnas so she can enjoy home cooked meals when she is alone.

Cool food quickly before placing it in the freezer. Sometimes the quality of the food will suffer if the food isn't room temperature or cooler when the freezing process begins. The longer it takes for a food item to freeze completely, the bigger the ice crystals will be in the finished product. You can cool food by putting it into the refrigerator for awhile, or fill the bottom of your sink with ice water and set the pans in the water until the food has cooled (stir the food to cool it more quickly). Some people who live in areas where it snows and gets below freezing during the winter will actually cool their food by placing it outside in a snow bank.

You don't want to put hot food directly into plastic freezer bags.

Pack your freezer containers tightly without air pockets, but remember to leave "head space" of at least one-inch allowing for the expansion of liquid-based meals.

Set meal packages directly onto freezer shelves allowing room for air circulation. After the meals are frozen solid, stack them tightly.

Remove air from your freezer bags by either pressing the air out with your hands, starting at the bottom and working upward, or by using a drinking straw to draw out excess air before sealing.

Label all freezer bags and containers with the name of the meal, date when it was frozen, number of servings, heating instructions, and any other special-preparation instructions, i.e. sprinkle with one cup grated cheese before baking, etc.

Package grated cheese or crumb toppings separately in small freezer bags and tape to the main-dish container. Be sure to include instructions on the label for adding the toppings or cheese when reheating at serving time.

CHAPTER THREE

Preparing Your Kitchen

A kitchen filled with a minimum amount of high-quality, multi-use items is easier to care for than a kitchen overflowing with single-use, low quality items. The following is a list of kitchen supplies that are handy to have around for a big cooking day.

NEED TO HAVE:

apron
baking dishes (9-inch square, 9''x13'', loaf pan)
baking sheets (two)
bowls (several of various sizes for holding ingredients during preparation)
bulb baster
cake pans (two 8-inch rounds, two 8-inch squares)
can opener (high quality hand can opener or electric)
casserole dishes with covers (2 quart, 3 quart)
colander
corkscrew
cutting board
grater
hot pads (at least two)
ladles (at least two)
kitchen scissors
kitchen towels (several)
knives (8-inch chef knife, paring knife, long serrated bread knife)
measuring cups (2 complete sets—one for dry, one for wet ingredients)
measuring spoons (two complete sets)
mixing bowls (set of three: small, medium and large)
muffin tins

pastry brush
pie pans
rolling pin
rubber gloves
rubber spatulas (assorted sizes)
saucepans (one large, one medium)
scrub brush
skillets (one large, one medium)
slotted spoons (made of reinforced nylon so they won't scratch pans)
soup pan with lid (the larger the better, preferably more than one)
spoons (several wooden spoons; and also several long handled stirring spoons)
tongs
vegetable peeler
vegetable steamer (wire basket that fits inside covered saucepan)
waterproof marking pen (Sharpie™ brand is best)
wire whisks (set of at least two different sizes)

NICE TO HAVE (BUT NOT NECESSARY):

blender
electric mixer (hand-held or free-standing)

electric skillet (frees up space on your stovetop burners)
electric wok
food processor
garlic press
ice cream scoop (for making meatballs and scooping cookie dough)
microwave oven
pizza pan
rice cooker
salad shooter (for grating cheese)
slow cooker (having two can be helpful)
tea kettle (for boiling water)

toaster
toaster oven

ODDS AND ENDS:
cupcake liners
foil (heavy-duty)
freezer bags (assorted sizes)
napkins
paper towels
extra permanent marking pen
plastic freezer containers (in various sizes)
plastic wrap, clear
waxed paper

PANTRY SUPPLIES:
(Don't run out and buy all these items in one shopping trip. As you go through your regular shopping and cooking processes, you'll find you've already stocked many of these items. If you add one or two additional items to your shopping list each payday, you'll quickly develop a well-stocked pantry.)

allspice
almonds (whole, sliced and slivered)
almond extract
artichoke hearts, marinated
artichoke hearts, plain
baking chocolate (unsweetened)
baking mix (such as Bisquick™)
baking powder
baking soda
basil
bay leaves
beans (canned and dried—black, kidney, pinto, white and lentils)
beef broth, canned
bouillon cubes or granules (chicken and beef)
bread crumbs
cashews
catsup

cayenne
celery seed
chicken (canned)
chicken broth, canned
chili powder
chili sauce
chocolate chips, semi-sweet
cilantro
cinnamon, ground
cinnamon, sticks
cloves, ground
cloves, whole
cocoa powder (unsweetened)
coconut, shredded
cooking oil
cooking spray
couscous
cornmeal
cornstarch
corn syrup

crackers (assorted)
croutons
cumin
currants, dried
curry powder
dill
dry milk
egg noodles
evaporated milk
fennel
flour
fruit (canned peaches, pears, oranges, applesauce, mixed fruit)
garlic, minced
garlic powder
garlic salt
gelatin and pudding mixes
ginger
gravy mix packets
green chilies
herb blend
honey
hot chocolate mix, instant
Italian seasoning
jams and jellies, assorted
lemon peel
lemon juice
lemon pepper
lime juice
mace, ground
maple extract
maple syrup
marjoram
mayonnaise
mint extract
mushrooms, canned (whole and sliced)
mustard (regular and Dijon-style)
mustard, dry
nutmeg
nuts (walnuts, almonds, pecans)
oatmeal, instant

oats, rolled
olive oil
olives, black (whole and sliced)
olives, green
onion powder
onion salt
oregano
paprika
Parmesan cheese, unopened
parsley flakes
pastas, assorted dry (spaghetti, fettuccine, manicotti shells, elbow macaroni, bow-ties, penne, rigatoni, small shells, large shells)
peanut butter
peanuts, in shell
peanuts, shelled
pectin
pepper, black
pepper, white
peppercorns, whole
pepper sauce (Tabasco)
pine nuts
pizza sauce
poppy seeds
powdered milk
raisins
red pepper flakes
rice, brown
rice, instant
rice, long grain
rice, white
rice, wild
rosemary
saffron
sage
salad dressing-mix packets
salsa
salt
sesame oil
sesame seeds
Sloppy Joe seasoning packets

soup, canned (tomato, chicken noodle, French onion, whatever else your family eats regularly)
soup, cream of (mushroom, chicken, broccoli, asparagus)
soup, dry mixes (chicken noodle, French onion)
soy sauce
spaghetti sauce, jars or cans
spaghetti sauce, mix packets
sunflower seeds, shelled
sugar, brown
sugar, powdered
sugar, white
sweetened condensed milk
taco seasoning packets
tarragon
texturized vegetable protein (TVP)
tomato juice
tomato paste
tomato sauce
tomatoes, crushed or diced
tomatoes, stewed (regular, diced, Italian-style and Mexican-style)
tomatoes, with green chilies
thyme
tuna
turmeric
vanilla extract
vegetables (assorted canned)
vegetable oil
vegetable shortening (solid)
vegetable broth, canned
vegetable soup mix packets
vinegar, balsamic
vinegar, cider
vinegar, red wine
vinegar, white
vinegar, white wine
walnuts (halves and chopped)
water chestnuts
wheat germ
wine, dry red

wine, dry white
Worcestershire sauce
yeast, active dry

REFRIGERATOR & FREEZER SUPPLIES:

butter
buttermilk
cheeses (Cheddar, Monterey Jack, mozzarella, Parmesan, ricotta, Romano, Swiss)
corn kernels, frozen
cottage cheese
cream, whipping
cream cheese
eggs
egg substitute
garlic cloves, whole
ginger root, whole
green beans, frozen
lemon juice
lima beans, frozen
lime juice
margarine
milk
mixed vegetables, frozen
Parmesan cheese, opened
peas, frozen
salad dressings (assorted)
sour cream
tortillas, corn
tortillas, flour
yogurt, plain

PRODUCE:
cabbage
carrots
celery
cilantro, fresh
garlic cloves
green onions
bell pepper, green
bell pepper, red
onions
parsley, fresh
potatoes
tofu

Breakfasts

Perfectly Pleasing Pancakes

6 servings

4 eggs
1 quart milk
3 tablespoons vanilla extract
4 tablespoons melted margarine
4 cups flour
¼ cup sugar
¼ cup baking powder
2 teaspoons salt
¾ cup vegetable oil
margarine (or cooking spray)

In a large bowl, beat eggs; add milk and vanilla and mix well. Add melted margarine and stir. Add dry ingredients and oil, mix well. Heat griddle or frying pan to medium. Melt a tad of butter in the pan. Ladle pancake batter onto griddle or pan by the spoonful. Brown lightly on each side.

To Freeze:
Store cooked pancakes in individual freezer bags.

To Serve:
Place frozen pancakes in toaster and toast on medium setting. Serve with butter and syrup or fruit preserves.

Pumpkin Custard

12 servings

13 egg whites
1½ cup Splenda™ (or other natural sweetener) or sugar
1 teaspoon cinnamon
½ teaspoon ginger
½ teaspoon nutmeg
½ teaspoon ground cloves
2 (12 ounce) cans fat-free condensed milk
1 (29 ounce) can pumpkin (not pumpkin pie filling)

Preheat oven to 350 degrees. Combine the egg whites, Splenda™ and spices in a large bowl. Beat with a mixer for 2 minutes. Add 1 can of condensed milk and beat 1 more minute. With the mixer still running, add all of the pumpkin and then the remaining can of condensed milk. Spray a large baking dish with cooking spray. Poor custard into dish. Bake for 1 hour.

To Freeze:
Bake partially for 30 minutes. Remove from heat and cover with foil. Freeze for up to one month.

To Serve:
Remove from freezer and let thaw overnight. Cook 30 minutes in a 350-degree oven or until heated through.

Notes from the Chef:
Easy to make, this is great for a high-energy breakfast or snack. Make it the night before. There is almost no fat, very few carbs and it's extremely high in both protein and vitamin A. If you substitute Splenda™ for sugar it is also sugar free! You can feel good about your kids eating this for breakfast and they'll love it! Serve hot or refrigerate overnight and serve cold (our preference).

Apple Pancakes

8 servings

1 cup flour
½ teaspoon salt
1 egg
1 cup milk
1 tablespoon vegetable oil
5 medium apples, peeled and thinly sliced

Combine flour and salt in a bowl. In a separate bowl, beat together egg, milk and oil. Combine wet and dry ingredients and stir until smooth. Fold in apples. Heat a frying pan, sprayed with cooking spray, over medium heat. Spoon batter into pan, making pancakes that are 4 to 5 inches round. Flip when bubbles begin to form on top. Cook until golden brown.

To Freeze:
Store cooked pancakes in individual freezer bags.

To Serve:
Place frozen pancakes in toaster and toast on medium setting. Serve with butter and syrup or fruit preserves.

Ham & Cheese Crêpes

8-10 servings

For Crêpes:
2 cups flour
2 cups milk
1 tablespoon salt
2 eggs

For Serving Day:
sliced-cooked ham
mustard
shredded cheese of your choice

To make crêpes combine all batter-ingredients in a blender or whisk in a metal mixing bowl. Spoon crêpe mixture into a frying pan, and use spoon to spread mixture till almost opaque. As soon as top appears slightly bubbly, flip and cook just until done.

To Freeze:
Stack crêpes between layers of waxed paper before putting into a freezer bag. Freeze for up to 3 months.

To Serve:
Thaw crêpes for 2-3 hours. Spread each with mustard, a slice of cooked ham, and a bit of cheese. Roll up tightly. Place in a non-stick sprayed baking dish and bake, uncovered, in a 350-degree oven for 12-16 minutes, or until heated through and cheese has melted.

Breakfast Pizza Sandwich

6 servings

6 eggs
5 tablespoons finely chopped green pepper
5 tablespoons milk
½teaspoon dried oregano
6 English muffins
⅛ cup pizza sauce
¾ cup crumbled breakfast sausage
⅛ cup shredded cheese of your choice

Combine eggs, green pepper, milk and oregano in a bowl. Cook egg mixture over medium heat in a skillet sprayed with cooking spray. Once eggs are set, remove from heat. Toast English muffins. Split toasted muffins in half and spread a small amount of pizza sauce on each half. Place egg mixture on sauce. Top with sausage and shredded cheese. Heat under a broiler for a few minutes to heat through and melt cheese.

To Freeze:
Prepare up to the point of adding cheese. Wrap individually in foil and freeze. Place a small amount of shredded cheese in a plastic bag and attach to breakfast sandwich.

To Serve:
Thaw for several hours. Sprinkle cheese on top of muffin. Bake for 20 minutes in a 350-degree oven. Broil for the last few minutes for a golden finish, if desired.

Blueberry French Toast Bake

12 servings

For French Toast:
16 slices white bread, crusts removed
2½ (8 ounce) packages cream cheese
1½ cups blueberries (fresh or frozen)
16 eggs
2½ cups milk
½ cup maple syrup

For Topping:
1¼ cups milk
2½ tablespoons cornstarch
1¼ cups water
1½ cups blueberries (fresh or frozen)

Cut bread into cubes and place ½ of the bread in the bottom of a 9x13-inch baking dish coated with cooking spray. Cut cream cheese into cubes and place on top of bread. Spread the blueberries over cream cheese. Top with remaining bread. Combine eggs, milk and syrup in a bowl. Pour over bread mixture. Cover with foil and chill overnight. Remove from refrigerator 30 minutes before baking. Leave covered and bake in a 350- degree oven for 30 minutes. Remove cover and bake an additional 30 minutes or until a toothpick inserted in the center comes out clean. In a saucepan combine sugar and cornstarch over medium heat. Add water. Bring to a boil until mixture begins to thicken. Stir in blueberries and reduce heat. Simmer for 7-10 minutes. Cut baked toast into serving-size squares and serve with sauce.

To Freeze:
Cook as directed above and let cool. Cut into serving-size squares, wrap with foil and freeze. Do not prepare sauce.

To Serve:
Thaw overnight. Bake in a 350-degree oven until heated through. While French toast is baking prepare sauce. Serve warm with sauce on top.

Sausage Strata

10 servings

1 pound turkey sausage
6 eggs
2 cups milk
1 teaspoon ground mustard
6 slices white bread, cubed
1 cup Cheddar cheese

Brown sausage in a skillet over medium heat. Drain and set aside. Combine eggs, milk and mustard in a large mixing bowl. Add bread cubes, cheese and sausage; toss well. Spray an 9 x 13-inch baking dish with cooking spray and pour mixture into dish. Refrigerate overnight. Remove from refrigerator 30 minutes before baking. Bake in a 350-degree oven for 40 minutes or until a knife inserted in the center comes out clean.

To Freeze:
Prepare as directed above and let cool. Cut into serving-size squares. Wrap in foil and freeze.

To Serve:
Thaw overnight. Bake in a 350-degree oven until heated through.

Spectacular Scones

10 servings

2 cups flour
1 tablespoon sugar
1 tablespoon baking powder
¼ teaspoon baking soda
½ teaspoon salt
3 tablespoons cold butter
½ cup diced dried fruit (your choice)
½ teaspoon grated orange peel
¾ cup buttermilk
milk (to coat)

Combine flour, sugar, baking powder, baking soda and salt in a bowl. Cut in butter until mixture is crumbly. Add fruit and orange peel. Stir in buttermilk. Stir until a soft dough forms. Turn dough onto a floured surface and knead for 3-4 minutes. Roll dough into a circle and cut into 10 wedges. Place wedges on a baking sheet coated with cooking spray. Brush each scone lightly with milk to prevent crumbling. Bake in a 425- degree oven for 15 minutes or until lightly browned.

To Freeze:
Cool. Wrap with foil or place in individual freezing bags. Label and freeze.

To Serve:
Thaw overnight. Warm slightly, if desired, in a microwave or 350-degree oven.

Simple Sandwiches

12 servings

12 English muffins, split, toasted and buttered
1 dozen eggs
12 bacon strips, cooked and drained
12 slices of Cheddar cheese

Scramble eggs in a large skillet or fry
individually on a griddle. Assemble each
sandwich with 1 English muffin, 1 egg,
1 strip of bacon (cut in half) and 1 slice of
cheese.

The Perfect Egg

If frying eggs
individually, use round
canning rings to force
eggs to maintain a round
shape.

To Freeze:
Wrap each sandwich individually in a paper towel, then place several
sandwiches in large zip-top freezer bag. Or wrap in foil to freeze
individually.

To Serve:
Microwave on high for 1-2 minutes or thaw sandwiches, re-wrap in foil and
bake in a 400-degree oven for 15-20 minutes.

Notes from the Chef...

Fat-free egg substitutes can be used in place of eggs. For another variation,
try homemade biscuits or store-bought biscuits in place of English muffins.
When using biscuits, undercook slightly for freezing or they will be too
crumbly during the final preparation. Canadian bacon, ham slices or
cooked sausage patties can be substituted for the bacon slices.

Breakfast Burritos

12 servings

6 eggs, beaten
½ pound sausage, cooked and crumbled
¼ cup chunky salsa, you choose the heat
1 cup shredded Cheddar cheese
12 flour tortillas

Scramble eggs in a large skillet until set. Stir in sausage and salsa. Warm tortillas in microwave for 20-30 seconds or until warm and flexible. Place ½ cup egg mixture onto tortilla; roll burrito-style.

To Freeze:
Freeze burritos in single layer on lightly greased cookie sheet. When fully frozen, wrap burritos individually. Place wrapped burritos in a large zip-top freezer bag and continue to freeze.

To Serve:
Cook in microwave until heated through, about 2 minutes. To bake, thaw burritos, wrap in foil and bake in a 350-degree oven for 10 minutes.

Notes from the Chef...
Be creative with your tortillas to jazz up your mornings. Try adding green onions, a peeled and chopped tomato, shredded potatoes or hashbrowns, jalapeno slices, minced garlic, chopped onion, peppers or whatever other ingredients your family loves!

Breakfast Bake

6 servings

4 ounces shredded Cheddar cheese
½ medium onion, chopped
⅛ cup chopped green pepper
⅛ cup chopped sweet red pepper
1 (4.5 ounce) can sliced mushrooms,
  drained
4 eggs
2 cups milk
½ teaspoon salt
6 bacon strips, cooked and crumbled
  (or ½ cup ham, diced)
2 cups seasoned croutons

Sprinkle croutons, onion, peppers, cheese
and mushrooms into an 8 x 8-inch baking
dish. Combine eggs, milk, salt and pepper
in a bowl and pour over crouton mixture.
Top with ham or bacon.

Less Mess, Less Dishes

You can easily conserve dishes and make easy and disposable storage containers with aluminum foil. Line your baking dish with foil. After cooking, freeze dish with foil, food and all. When frozen, carefully lift from dish. Wrap with more foil, label, date and return to freezer.

To Freeze:
Cover and freeze for up to 3 months.

To Serve:
Thaw for 24 hours prior to serving. Remove from refrigerator ½ hour prior
to baking. Bake, uncovered, at 350 degrees for 45-55 minutes or until a
knife inserted in center comes out clean.

Soups & Sides

Chicken Tortellini Soup

6 servings

1 cup thinly sliced carrots
½ cup chopped onion
½ cup thinly sliced celery
1 cup chicken-breast meat, cooked and cut into ½-inch cubes
6 cups reduced-fat chicken broth (reserved from cooking chicken or canned)
1 cup cheese-filled tortellini, dried and uncooked
½ teaspoon thyme leaves, dried
¼ teaspoon black pepper
1 bay leaf
2 tablespoons snipped fresh parsley

Cook chicken the night before; reserve broth. Cut chicken into ½-inch cubes. Slice carrots and celery. Chop onion. Using broth reserved from cooking chicken the night before, bring broth to a boil; add carrots, onion, celery, thyme, black pepper and bay leaf. Cover; simmer over medium-low heat for 15 minutes. Cool. Remove bay leaf. Add cubed chicken, uncooked pasta and fresh parsley.

To Freeze:

Place in labeled freezer bags; seal and freeze.

To Serve:

Thaw. Heat over medium heat, covered, for 15 minutes or until pasta is cooked and tender.

Asparagus Potato Soup

20 servings

3½ pounds asparagus, trimmed and cut into 1-inch lengths
3-4 large baking potatoes, peeled and cut into ½-inch cubes
3-4 medium yellow onions, peeled and cut into slim wedges
12 cups chicken broth
¾ teaspoon ground mace
½ teaspoon ground nutmeg
1-2 teaspoons salt, or to taste
1 teaspoon freshly ground pepper
7 shakes McCormick's Season-all™
20 tablespoons freshly grated Parmesan cheese.

Place all ingredients, except cheese, in large saucepan. Bring the liquid to a simmer over moderate heat then adjust the heat so the soup bubbles gently. Cover the pot and simmer for 30 to 35 minutes, until the vegetables are very tender. Cool the soup still covered for 20 minutes. Purêe the broth and vegetables in batches, in a blender or food processor fitted with metal chopping blade.

To Freeze:
Cool. Place in freezer-safe containers, label and freeze. Freeze parmesan cheese in a zip-top bag and attach to soup, along with labeled instructions.

To Serve:
Thaw puree and heat over moderate heat to serving temperature. Ladle the soup into heated bowls and top each portion with 1 tablespoon of parmesan cheese.

Chicken Noodle Soup

6 servings

1 teaspoon vegetable oil
2 cups chopped onion
8 cups reduced-fat chicken broth
3 cloves garlic, minced
½ teaspoon thyme
¼ teaspoon pepper
2 large carrots, thinly sliced
½ cup chopped celery
5 ounces dried wide egg noodles
1 pound boneless-chicken breast meat, cut into
  cubes
1 medium-sized tomato, seeded and chopped
1 medium zucchini, sliced
1 teaspoon salt
2 tablespoons chopped parsley

Soup too Salty?

If you find your soup too salty, thinly slice a potato and add it to the soup for 10-15 minutes. The potato will help absorb extra salt in the broth. Don't forget to remove it before serving!

Cut chicken into ½-inch cubes. Chop onions, celery and parsley. Seed and chop tomatoes. Mince garlic. Slice carrots and zucchini. In large pan or Dutch oven, heat oil over medium heat. Add onion and cook until softened, stirring frequently. Stir in broth, garlic, thyme, pepper, carrots, celery and chicken. Reduce heat to low; cover and simmer until carrots are barely tender and chicken is no longer pink (less than 10 minutes). Remove from heat. Stir in zucchini, tomato and parsley. If serving immediately, add noodles and cook until noodles are tender.

To Freeze:
Do not add noodles. Instead, remove from heat and cool. Pour into labeled freezer bag; freeze. Attach uncooked noodles in separate bag, along with directions for finishing soup.

To Serve:
Thaw. Place in large pan or Dutch oven; add noodles. Heat over medium heat until heated through and noodles are cooked and tender.

Country-Beef Soup

6 servings

6 cups water
3 cups canned, Italian-style stewed tomatoes (cut up and liquid reserved)
1 pound potatoes, peeled and cut into ½-inch cubes
1 pound cooked beef, diced
1½ cups sliced celery
1½ cups sliced mushrooms
1½ cups sliced carrots
1 cup chopped onion
1 cup frozen whole-kernel corn
6 packets instant-beef broth and seasoning mix
2 tablespoons parsley
1 teaspoon pepper

Dice beef; sauté in large skillet until cooked through. Peel potatoes; cut into ½-inch cubes; store in large pan of cold water in refrigerator until ready to use. Slice celery, mushrooms and carrots. Chop onion. Combine all ingredients in large stockpot or Dutch oven. Heat to a boil and cook until potatoes are tender.

To Freeze:
Remove from heat just before potatoes are tender and cool quickly. Pour into labeled freezer bags. Freeze.

To Serve:
Thaw; heat in Dutch oven over medium-high heat until heated through and potatoes are tender.

Sunshine Soup

6 servings

1 can vegetable broth
1 can creamed corn
1 small onion, chopped
1 clove garlic, chopped
1 teaspoon cumin
1 teaspoon coriander
1 tablespoon olive oil
1 sweet potato, peeled and cubed into ¾-inch cubes
1 can whole corn or 1 cup frozen corn
2 carrots, chopped

Sauté onion and garlic in olive oil in the bottom of the soup pot. Add broth, creamed corn, cumin and coriander. Simmer for 20 minutes. Add the rest of the vegetables you want to freeze (see chef note). Simmer 10 minutes longer.

To Freeze:
Cool and pour into freezer-safe containers. Label and freeze.

To Serve:
Defrost and heat, adding sweet potato, corn, and carrots if they haven't been added earlier. Note that sweet potato takes a few minutes to cook, so cooking time will be longer if you have chosen to add it when reheating.

Notes from the Chef...
You can freeze this soup with all the ingredients included, or if you want a crunchier soup with more texture, you can add the whole corn and carrots when reheating. The sweet potato can also be added during reheating although it takes a bit more time to prepare.

Snappy Black Bean Soup

6 servings

2 cups black beans, rinsed and soaked overnight
2 tablespoons olive oil
1 onion, chopped
2 cloves of garlic, pressed
2 teaspoons cumin
2 cups chicken broth
1 cup jarred salsa

In a crock pot, place your soaked black beans. In a skillet, heat oil and sauté onion and garlic together for 3 minutes or until onion is soft. Add this mixture to the crock pot. Then, add cumin and chicken broth and cook on low all day -about 8 hours. Stir in the salsa just before serving. You can serve this delicious soup topped with sour cream and green onions, if you like.

To Freeze:
To freeze, simply cool and store in freezer-safe containers, label and date.

To Serve:
Thaw and warm over medium heat until heated through.

Recipe by Leanne Ely, author of *The Frantic Family Cookbook* and *Healthy Foods*.

Separate Your Soup

To separate fats from soup, try using a fat-separator cup. Like a tea pot, soup stock pours through the spout leaving the fat behind. A great gadget to add to your kitchen collection!

Turkey Green-Chile Soup

6 servings

3 teaspoons olive oil
12 ounces lean ground turkey
2 large leeks, cleaned and sliced
2 large celery ribs, chopped
9 baby carrots, chopped
1 cup green chilies, chopped (medium heat)
7½ cups chicken stock
1 cup evaporated skim milk
1½ cups chopped onion
salt and pepper to taste

For serving day:
Cooked-brown rice, canned hominy, or cooked and cubed potatoes,
(all optional, but flavor enhancing to the final dish)

In a large sauté pan cook onion and leek in olive oil until tender, about 3
minutes. Transfer to soup pot and add 6 cups of the chicken stock and the
green chilies. Simmer for 10 minutes. Remove from heat, puree, and add
back to soup pot. In original sauté pan cook ground turkey until no longer
pink. Add carrots and celery. Cook for 2 minutes over high heat to get a
little color on meat and veggies. Add in the remaining stock and cover.
Cook for 5 minutes. Add meat mixture to soup pot along with salt and
pepper to taste. Blend all and serve.

To Freeze:
Cool and place in plastic containers, label and date.

To Serve:
Warm in microwave oven or on stove top until heated; then stir in the rice,
hominy or potatoes, if desired.

Notes from the Chef...
This is a wonderful soup to keep on hand! Serve each bowl with ½ cup
cooked brown rice or the same amount of canned hominy or cooked
potato cubes. This soup tastes amazing if you get the balance of flavor and
heat from the chilies just right.

Broccoli-Cheese Soup

6 servings

6 cups chicken broth (or water with chicken bouillon granules)
2 (10 ounce) packages frozen cut broccoli
¼ cup chopped onion
½ cup butter
⅔ cup flour
1 cup whipping cream
3½ cups shredded Cheddar cheese

For Serving Day:
bread bowls (optional)

Combine chicken broth, broccoli and onion in a large saucepan or Dutch oven. Bring to boiling, reduce heat and simmer uncovered for 10 minutes. Melt margarine in a small saucepan and stir in flour until mixture is smooth. Add to the larger pan and continue cooking while stirring constantly, blending well, for about 5 minutes. Stir in the cream and Cheddar cheese until the cheese melts.

To Freeze:
Cool. Place in freezer-safe containers, label and freeze.

To Serve:
Thaw. Warm over medium heat until heated through. Scoop into bread bowls.

Notes from the Chef...
This is especially delicious when served in bread bowls.

Apple Barley Soup

20 Servings

7 large onions, thinly sliced
7 tablespoons vegetable oil
12 cups vegetable stock
5 cups apple cider
1-2 cups pearl barley
7 large carrots, diced
4 teaspoons thyme
5 teaspoons dried marjoram
3 bay leaves
5-6 teaspoons McCormick's Season-all™
7 cups unpeeled-chopped apples
scant cup minced fresh parsley
3½ tablespoons lemon juice

In a large soup pot sauté onions in oil over medium heat for 5 minutes, stirring constantly. Reduce heat, cover and cook, stirring frequently for 10 minutes more, or until onions are browned. Add stock, cider, barley, carrots, thyme, marjoram, bay leaves and Season-all. Cover and cook for one hour or until barley is tender. Add apples, parsley and lemon juice. Cook for 5 minutes or until apples are tender and slightly soft but not mushy. Discard bay leaf.

To Freeze:
Cool. Place in freezer-safe containers, label and freeze.

To Serve:
Remove from freezer and heat to serving temperature.

Meatball Soup

6 servings

1 pound ground beef
½ cup bread crumbs
⅓ cup grated Romano cheese, divided
3 teaspoons oregano, divided
salt and pepper to taste
3 cans beef broth (or equivalent of homemade)
1 (28 ounce) can Italian-style tomatoes
6 carrots, diced
4 medium potatoes, peeled and diced
2 small onions, chopped
6 large garlic cloves, chopped
2 teaspoons thyme

Combine ground beef, bread crumbs, ½ of the grated Romano cheese, 1 teaspoon oregano, salt and pepper to taste in large bowl and blend well. Wet your hands and shape mixture into little meatballs, about 1-inch in diameter. In a Dutch oven, heat 1 tablespoon of the oil over medium-high heat. Cook onions, garlic and carrots till soft, about 3 minutes. Add beef broth to the Dutch oven and bring to a boil over high heat. Drop in the meatballs and cook 5 minutes. Add canned tomatoes, thyme and remaining 2 teaspoons oregano. Reduce heat to medium. Simmer soup about forty minutes uncovered, until meatballs and vegetables are cooked through and tender, breaking up tomatoes with back of spoon. Adjust seasoning to taste with salt and pepper. Ladle soup into bowls. Sprinkle with remaining Romano cheese and serve.

To Freeze:
To freeze, simply cool and store in freezer-safe containers, label and date.

To Serve:
Thaw and warm over medium heat until heated through.

* Recipe by Leanne Ely, author of *Healthy Foods* and *The Frantic Family Cookbook*

Country Cornbread Muffins

18 servings

3 cups self-rising flour
4 cups cornmeal
1 egg
3 cups skim milk
2¼ cups canned corn, drained
4 tablespoons sugar
3 tablespoons chopped green chilies

Preheat oven to 400 degrees. Combine self-rising flour and cornmeal in a plastic bag and shake until well blended. Combine eggs, sugar and milk in a bowl and beat until blended and sugar dissolved. Gradually add flour mixture and continue to blend until well-mixed. Fold in corn and chilies. Spray two muffins pans (utilizing 18 muffin wells) with cooking spray. Bake for 15-20 minutes until toothpick inserted in center comes out clean.

To Freeze:
Wrap individual muffins in foil and freeze or place in freezer bags. Label, date and freeze.

To Serve:
Thaw muffins in refrigerator. Heat in microwave 20 seconds to remove chill and warm slightly.

Mushroom-Chicken Couscous

6 servings

1 pound skinless, boneless chicken breasts
1 tablespoon margarine
1 large onion, finely chopped
8 ounces sliced mushrooms
2 teaspoons cornstarch
¼ cup reduced-fat chicken broth
3 tablespoons sherry
2 tablespoons soy sauce
⅛ teaspoon cayenne

For Serving Day:
2 cups skim milk
¾ cup reduced-fat chicken broth
1½ cups couscous
cooking spray
fresh cilantro sprigs (optional)

Maximize Your Mushrooms

Use mushrooms within 3-4 days of purchase for maximum taste and flavor. To maximize freshness, keep mushrooms stored inside a brown paper bag in your refrigerator.

Place chicken between sheets of plastic wrap or wax paper. Pound with a meat mallet until ¼-inch thick. Cut chicken into ½-inch wide strips. Chop onion. Slice mushrooms. In medium bowl, stir together cornstarch, ¼ cup broth, soy sauce, cayenne and sherry. In large skillet or saucepan, melt margarine over medium-high heat. Add onion and mushrooms; cook until onion is golden brown, stirring frequently; remove from heat. Remove onion mixture from skillet; set aside. Spray saucepan with cooking spray and place over medium-high heat; add chicken. Cook, stirring gently and frequently, until chicken is no longer pink. Add onion-mushroom mixture to cooked chicken; pour in cornstarch mixture and stir constantly over medium-high heat until sauce is thickened slightly and bubbly.

To Freeze:
Remove from heat. Cool. Place in freezer bag; label and freeze.

To Serve:
Thaw chicken mixture. In large saucepan, stir together milk and remaining broth; heat to boiling. Stir in couscous, cover pan and remove from heat; let sit for 10 minutes until liquid is absorbed. Heat chicken mixture over medium heat in large skillet until heated through. Fluff couscous. Serve chicken beside couscous. Garnish with cilantro.

Confetti Potatoes

6 servings

½ cup chopped green onions
1 (16 ounce) package frozen hash brown potatoes
1 (10 ounce) can Healthy Request™ Cream of Mushroom Soup
1 soup can skim milk
1 cup shredded fat-free Cheddar or mozzarella cheese
1 cup crumbled reduced-fat cheese crackers (like Cheese Nips™), divided
8-12 ounces of lean diced ham, cooked diced chicken, or cooked diced
    turkey (meat is optional)

Mix hash browns, soup and milk together in a large bowl. Add cheese, onions, and ½ cup cheese crackers. Add meat, if using. Pour into 9 x 13-inch casserole dish and top with remaining cracker crumbs.

To Freeze:
Cover with foil, label and freeze.

To Serve:
Thaw and bake in a 375-degree oven for 35 minutes or until heated through.

Chicken-Mushroom Rolls

6 servings

2 cups sliced mushrooms
4 teaspoons margarine
4 teaspoons flour
1 cup reduced-fat chicken broth
1 teaspoon lemon juice
½ cup chopped onion
½ cup chopped celery
½ cup chopped green bell pepper
2 garlic cloves, minced
2 ounces onion and garlic-flavored croutons
2 eggs, beaten
6 boneless-chicken breasts, pounded thin

Pound chicken breasts with meat mallet until very thin. Chop onion, celery and green pepper. Slice mushrooms. Mince garlic. In large skillet, melt ½ the margarine (2 teaspoons). Add onion, celery, green pepper and garlic; sauté until softened. Remove from heat. In another skillet, melt 2 teaspoons margarine. Stir in mushrooms and cook until softened. Sprinkle flour over mushrooms; stir constantly over medium heat for 1 minute. Add broth and lemon juice to mushrooms. Cook for 2 additional minutes. Remove from heat. Stir croutons and beaten eggs into onion/celery/green pepper mixture. Spread vegetable/crouton mixture onto center of each pounded chicken breast. Roll each chicken breast and secure with a toothpick and place seam-side down in 9 x 13-inch baking dish. If serving immediately, cover with mushroom sauce and bake for 45 minutes in a 350-degree oven or until chicken is cooked through.

To Freeze:
Do not bake. Cover chicken roll pan; label and freeze. Pour mushroom sauce into separate labeled freezer bag; attach to chicken-roll pan; freeze.

To Serve:
Thaw. Stir mushroom sauce to re-combine. Add a small amount of water or chicken broth if too thick. Pour mushroom sauce over top of chicken rolls. Tightly cover pan and bake at 350 degrees for 45 minutes until chicken is cooked through.

All-Day Fix & Forget Chili

6-8 servings

½ pound ground beef
½ pound ground sausage
2-3 tablespoons taco seasoning
1 can pinto beans, drained
1 can kidney beans, drained
1 can black beans, drained
1 can whole kernel corn, drained
2 cans Mexican stewed tomatoes (chop the tomatoes a little)
2 (4 ounce) cans diced green chilies
½ medium onion, chopped
1 green bell pepper, chopped
2 fresh garlic cloves, minced (or more to taste)
2 teaspoons cumin (or to taste)
1 teaspoon garlic salt
1 tablespoon oregano
1 tablespoon sugar
1-2 teaspoons chili powder (or more to taste)
salt and pepper to taste

Brown both meats, drain off fat, add taco seasoning, and simmer 10 minutes. Put all ingredients into crock pot. Add all spices and seasonings. Simmer all day on low setting. Serve.

Optional Chili Toppings

green onions,
Monterey Jack cheese
Cheddar cheese
red onions
guacamole
sour cream
salsa
jalapenos

To Freeze:
Simply cool and freeze in freezer-safe containers.

To Serve:
Simply thaw and warm over medium heat until heated through.

Notes from the Chef...

This chili is great over a baked potato, good on chili dogs, or also wrapped in flour tortillas for chili burritos. You can also try it over a bed of corn chips for nachos, or with lettuce and tortilla chips for taco salad. This recipe is simple to double for freezing and it freezes great for months!

Make Mine Mashed (Potatoes)

8 servings

5 pounds of potatoes, peeled and quartered
1 egg
1 tablespoon minced garlic
½ teaspoon pepper
1 teaspoon salt
6 ounces sour cream
Shredded cheese of your choice (optional)
¼ cup butter, melted

Cook potatoes in boiling water until tender. Drain. Combine all ingredients except cheese and butter in a large mixing bowl. Mix or mash well. Spoon potatoes into a 9 x 13-inch casserole dish coated with cooking spray, or use disposable aluminum pans. Warm butter in a saucepan over low heat, being careful not to scorch. Drizzle over potatoes.

To Freeze:
Cover and freeze. If using cheese, place in a zip-top bag and attach to potato dish.

To Serve:
Thaw. Warm in a 375-degree oven for 40 minutes or until heated through. Sprinkle cheese on top and continue cooking until cheese has just melted.

Entrees

Chicken-Asparagus Crustless Quiche

6 servings

2 cups asparagus, cut into 1-inch
pieces
2 tablespoons flour
½ teaspoon salt
¼ teaspoon black pepper
pinch cayenne
1 cup chicken breast meat,
cooked and cubed
2 teaspoons vegetable oil

½ cup finely chopped red bell
pepper
½ cup chopped onion
1 cup skim milk
3 eggs (or one cup egg
substitute)
4 ounces (1 cup) reduced-fat
Cheddar cheese, grated

Cook chicken; cut into ½-inch pieces. Chop bell pepper and onion. Cut asparagus spears into 1-inch pieces. Grate cheese. Cook asparagus just until tender. Drain and rinse. In skillet, heat oil over medium-high heat. Cook red bell pepper and onion 5 minutes or until soft. Remove from heat. Stir in chicken, salt, pepper and cayenne. In large bowl, whisk together milk, eggs and 2 tablespoons flour until frothy. Stir in cheese, asparagus and chicken-vegetable mixture. Stir to combine.

To Freeze:
Pour into labeled freezer bag; seal and freeze.

To Serve:
Thaw completely. Squeeze bag gently to re-combine quiche mixture. Preheat oven to 350 degrees. Spray 9-inch pie plate or quiche pan with cooking spray. Pour quiche mixture into pie plate. Bake 45 minutes, or until knife inserted near center comes out clean. Let stand 10 minutes before serving. Slice into 6 equal wedge-shaped servings.

Cacciatore Penne

6 servings

2 cups chicken breast meat,
   cooked and cubed
1 cup canned reduced-fat chicken
   broth
1 small green bell pepper, thinly
   sliced
1 (8 ounce) package whole
   mushrooms, halved

2 (14.5 ounce) cans diced
   tomatoes with Italian
   seasonings, (with liquid)
10 ounces (2 cups) uncooked
   penne pasta

For Serving Day:
¼ cup Parmesan cheese

Cook chicken; cut into cubes. Slice green pepper. Halve mushrooms. Cook pasta according to package directions until just tender. Rinse in cold water; place in large pan of cold water; store in refrigerator until ready to use. In large skillet combine broth, sliced green bell pepper, mushrooms and tomatoes. Cook over medium-high heat until green pepper slices are tender and mushrooms are cooked through. Remove from heat. Stir in chicken and drained pasta.

To Freeze:
Pour into labeled freezer bags; seal and freeze.

To Serve:
Thaw completely. Reheat in large skillet until heated through. Serve hot, sprinkled with Parmesan cheese.

Noodle Heaven

6 servings

1 pound lean ground beef
2 cloves garlic, minced
1 teaspoon salt
1 teaspoon sugar
2 (8 ounce) cans tomato sauce
1 (8 ounce) package of cream cheese, softened
1 cup low-fat sour cream
5 green onions, chopped
1 (8 ounce) package noodles of your choice
1 cup Cheddar cheese, grated

Brown beef in a large skillet. Add garlic, salt, sugar and tomato sauce and simmer 10 minutes or until meat is lightly browned. In a small bowl blend cream cheese, sour cream and onions. Boil noodles, undercooking a minute or two; drain. In a 9 x 13-inch baking dish, layer noodles, the cream cheese mixture and meat sauce. Repeat layers. Sprinkle Cheddar cheese on top.

To Freeze:
Cover with foil, label and freeze.

To Serve:
Transfer to refrigerator the night before. Bake in a 350-degree oven for 40 minutes, or until heated through and cheese is melted and bubbly.

Chicken, Cheese
& Mushroom Crêpes

8 servings

For Crêpes:
2 cups milk
2 cups flour

2 eggs
2 teaspoons salt

Combine all the ingredients with a whisk or blender, until smooth. Spray a nonstick pan with cooking spray and let warm over medium heat. Pour batter by spoonfuls into pan, swirling quickly and spreading with spoon to just cover the pan's surface. When edges are dry and underside cooked, flip and cook other side for 20-30 seconds.

To Freeze:
Stack crêpes with wax paper between each in a freezer bag.

For Filling:
1 tablespoon margarine
1 cup diced onion
3 cups sliced fresh mushrooms
1 cup shredded Swiss cheese (or Cheddar)

2½ cups chicken broth
1½ cups cooked chicken, diced
½ teaspoon pepper

Sauté onion in butter until soft. Add mushrooms and cook until tender. Remove onions and mushrooms, leaving juices in pan. Add flour to juices and cook, stirring constantly until thickened. Whisk in chicken broth and bring to a boil. Return onion and mushroom mixture to pan then reduce heat and let simmer for 5-10 minutes. Add chicken and seasoning and simmer for several more minutes. Remove from heat and stir in cheese.

To Freeze:
Cool the filling and divide into freezer bags.

To Serve:
Transfer filling to refrigerator the night before serving. Remove crêpes from freezer 45 minutes prior to serving. Preheat oven to 400 degrees. Spoon filling into crêpes, roll up and place seam-side down in baking dish sprayed with nonstick cooking spray. Bake until heated through and crêpes are lightly browned, 15 to 20 minutes

Marvelously Moist Meat Loaf

1 loaf

1½ pounds lean ground beef
⅓ cup dry breadcrumbs
2 eggs
½ cup chopped onion
1 teaspoons basil leaves
½ teaspoon salt
¼ teaspoon pepper

For Serving Day:
2 tablespoons Dijon style mustard
2 tablespoons honey

Mix the ground beef, breadcrumbs, eggs, onion, and seasonings in a large mixing bowl. Mix well. Add mustard and honey and mix in well. Shape into a loaf and place in pan to bake or freeze.

To Freeze:
Wrap in foil—or cook partially and then complete the cooking process after thawing. If completing the cooking process after thawing, make sure to write down the instructions on the foil of how many minutes are left for complete cooking. *Instructions: Mix the mustard and honey together to form a sauce. Spread sauce over loaf for the last 20minutesof cooking.*

To Serve:
One to two days prior to serving, transfer meat loaf to refrigerator to thaw. Bake the meat loaf for 30-40 minutes in a 350-degree oven. Spread honey-mustard sauce over top of meatloaf. Return to oven and bake for an additional 20 minutes or until cooked through and no longer pink.

Super-Quick Steak

6 servings

2 pounds steak (your choice)
6 tablespoons vinegar
3 tablespoons Worcestershire sauce
2 tablespoons olive oil
4 garlic cloves, minced

Cut steak into serving-size fillets, strips or bite-sized pieces—whatever your preference. Combine all ingredients, except steak, in a zipable freezer bag. Squeeze bag to mix. Add steak and mix again.

To Freeze:
Seal bag, label and freeze.

To Serve:
Remove meat from freezer the night before cooking and thaw, in marinade bag, in the refrigerator. Grill steak under oven broiler until desired doneness or use in beef dishes or serve over noodles.

Simple Spinach Enchiladas

6 servings

8 cups chopped fresh spinach
¾ cup shredded Cheddar cheese
6 flour tortillas

For serving day:
2½ cups enchilada sauce, divided
¾ cup shredded Cheddar cheese

Steam spinach 2-4 minutes, until just wilted and drain well. Pour 1 cup enchilada sauce in a 9 x 13-inch casserole dish coated with cooking spray. Divide spinach and ¾ cup of the cheese among tortillas. Roll tortillas and place seam side down in pan. Top with remaining sauce and cheese. Bake 15 minutes in a 400-degree oven or until lightly browned.

To Freeze:
Prepare enchiladas with spinach and cheese as directed above, but instead of placing in a baking dish, wrap with foil, label and freeze.

To Serve:
Spread 1 cup of enchilada sauce in the bottom of a 9 x 13-inch casserole dish coated with cooking spray. Place enchiladas in pan and top with remaining sauce and ¾ cup cheese. Bake in a 400-degree oven for 25-30 minutes or until lightly browned and heated thoroughly.

Cheese and Chicken Shells

6 servings

12 jumbo shell macaroni
1 egg, beaten
½ cup fat-free cottage cheese (or fat-free ricotta)
1 cup shredded, cooked chicken
2 ounces reduced-fat mozzarella cheese, grated
½ cup grated carrot
1 clove garlic, minced
¼ teaspoon salt
pepper to taste
1¾ cups skim milk
2 tablespoons cornstarch
4 ounces reduced-fat Swiss cheese, grated
¼ teaspoon nutmeg

Cook chicken; shred (for total of 1 cup). Cook macaroni shells according to package directions. Rinse in cold water to stop the cooking process. Grate mozzarella and Swiss cheeses. Grate carrots. In mixing bowl, combine beaten egg, cottage cheese, shredded chicken, mozzarella cheese, grated carrot, garlic, salt and pepper. Spoon into cooked pasta shells. In medium saucepan, combine milk and cornstarch; cook and stir until thickened and bubbly. Add Swiss cheese and nutmeg, stirring until cheese is melted. Place stuffed shells into freezer-safe pan. Spoon sauce evenly over shells.

To Freeze:
Cover with foil; label and freeze.

To Serve:
Thaw overnight in refrigerator . Bake in 350-degree oven for 30 minutes or until heated through. Sprinkle with a small amount of nutmeg.

Turkey Tetrazzini

6 servings

10 ounces spaghetti noodles
2 tablespoons reduced-fat
chicken broth
3 cups sliced mushrooms
1 cup chopped onion
¼ teaspoon thyme
½ teaspoon salt
½ teaspoon pepper
4 tablespoons flour

3 cups skim milk
1 cup canned fat-free chicken
broth
½ cup dry white wine
2 cups turkey meat, cooked and
cubed
¼ cup Parmesan cheese
3 tablespoons parsley

Roast and cube turkey. Slice mushrooms. Chop onion. Prepare spaghetti noodles according to package directions until just barely tender; drain and rinse in cold water. Place cooked noodles in large bowl of cold water in refrigerator until ready to use. In large skillet, heat 2 tablespoons chicken broth; add mushrooms, onion, thyme, salt and pepper. Cook over medium heat, stirring frequently, until mushrooms are golden brown (about 5 minutes). Stir flour, milk and broth into mushroom mixture; cook, until slightly thickened stirring constantly (about 1 minute). Remove from heat. Stir in wine. Place turkey and cooked-spaghetti noodles into large bowl; pour mushroom mixture over turkey and pasta; toss to combine. Spray 9 x 13-inch casserole dish with nonstick cooking spray. Transfer mixture to prepared dish; sprinkle with parsley and Parmesan cheese.

To Freeze:
Cool. Cover with foil; label and freeze.

To Serve:
Preheat oven to 375 degrees. Bake uncovered 25-35 minutes, or until lightly browned and bubbling.

Deep Dish Pizza Casserole

6 servings

2 cans refrigerated crescent rolls
1 (8 ounce) can tomato sauce
1 pound ground beef
1 small onion, chopped
2 cloves garlic minced
1 package pepperoni slices
1 small can mushrooms, drained
¼ cup chopped green pepper
¼ cup sliced black olives
2-3 cups mozzarella cheese, shredded and
  divided

Great Grater Trick

Tired of endlessly scrubbing your cheese grater? Make cleaning a breeze by spraying your grater with a non-stick cooking spray) before using.

Preheat oven to 350 degrees. Spray 9 x 13 -inch pan with cooking spray. Unroll 1 can of crescent rolls and press into pan. Brown ground beef with onions and garlic. Drain off fat. Mix with tomato sauce. Spread over crescent rolls in pan. Sprinkle 1 cup of cheese over ground beef. Layer pepperoni slices over cheese. Sprinkle mushrooms, green pepper, and olives over pepperoni. Sprinkle on the remaining cheese. Cover with the remaining package of crescent rolls. Bake at 350 degrees 20-30 minutes or until browned and heated through.

To Freeze:
Cook casserole for 10 minutes, then remove and cool. Cover with foil, label and freeze, along with final cooking directions.

To Serve:
Transfer from freezer to refrigerator to thaw. Preheat oven to 350 degrees. Cook 30-40 minutes or until browned and heated through.
.

Champion Chicken Tenders

6 servings

½ cup flour
1 teaspoon garlic powder, divided
1½ pounds chicken tenders
1 egg, beaten
1½ cups chicken broth

For serving day:
Dipping sauce (barbecue, ranch,
   honey-mustard)

Soup Separations

Flour and cornstarch may
separate soup when frozen.
To avoid this add ingredients
that thicken soup during the
reheating process.

Combine flour and ½ of garlic powder in a shallow bowl and mix well. Dip chicken into egg and then dredge in flour mixture. Brown chicken tenders in a nonstick skillet coated with cooking spray over medium heat for 6-8 minutes or until cooked through and no longer pink.

To Freeze:
Place in zipper top freezer bags. Label, date and freeze.

To Serve:
Microwave on high for 3 minutes. Serve with choice of sauce.

Turkey & Asparagus Strata

8 servings

2 tablespoons reduced-fat
  chicken broth
2 cups turkey meat, cooked and
  cubed
3 garlic cloves, minced
1 medium onion, chopped
1 cup thinly sliced asparagus
10 slices of bread (white or
  wheat) crusts removed, cut into
  4 triangles each

3 cups skim milk
4 eggs
¼ cup flour
1 teaspoon Dijon mustard
½ teaspoon salt
¼ teaspoon pepper
½ cup reduced-fat Cheddar
  cheese, grated

Cook and cube turkey meat. Mince garlic. Chop onion. Slice asparagus. Grate Cheddar cheese. In medium saucepan of boiling water, cook asparagus 3 minutes, until just tender. Drain, discarding liquid; rinse under cold running water until cool. Drain again. In large skillet, heat chicken broth; add onion and garlic. Cook over medium-high heat, stirring frequently until onion is tender. Transfer cooked onion to bowl; add cooked turkey and cooked asparagus; toss to combine. Spray 9x13-inch baking dish with nonstick cooking spray. In bottom of baking dish, layer bread triangles followed by turkey mixture. In separate medium-sized bowl, beat together milk, eggs, flour, mustard, salt and pepper; pour over turkey and bread layers. Sprinkle evenly with grated Cheddar cheese.

To Freeze:
Cover pan with foil; label and freeze.

To Serve:
Thaw. Preheat oven to 350 degrees. Bake 40 minutes, until mixture is set and cheese is melted and lightly browned.

Crockpot Stroganoff

6 servings

2 pounds of stew meat, cubed
¼ cup flour
olive oil
6 (10.75 ounce) cans cream of mushroom soup
2 (10.75 ounce) cans cream of celery soup
1 (16 ounce) container sour cream

For Serving Day:
rice or noodles, cooked fresh at time of serving

Dredge the stew meat through the flour and brown in hot cooking oil in a frying pan. Place the browned meat in a crock pot. Open all of the soups and pour them into the crockpot. Stir, then cover and let cook on low for 8-10 hours or until the meat is very tender. Stir in the sour cream and cook for 30 more minutes. Serve over hot noodles or rice.

To Freeze:
Do not prepare rice or noodles. Ladle stroganoff into containers and freeze. Mark a box of dry pasta in your pantry for this dish so that when you go to prepare it, you'll have all your needed ingredients.

To Serve:
Choose rice or noodles and cook according to package directions. Remove stroganoff from freezer and warm in a Dutch oven over medium heat or until heated through.

Old Fashioned Chicken & Rice

6 servings

2½ cups canned fat-free chicken broth
1½ pounds boneless skinless chicken breasts, cut into 1-inch pieces
1½ cups long-grain rice, uncooked
1 cup chopped onions

¼ cup minced fresh parsley
6 garlic cloves, minced
1 small red bell pepper, sliced into thin strips
1 (6 ounce) jar sliced mushrooms, with liquid
1 teaspoon poultry seasoning

Cut up chicken into 1-inch pieces. Chop onions. Mince garlic cloves and parsley. Slice red bell pepper into long thin strips. In large saucepan or Dutch oven, bring broth to a boil. Add remaining ingredients. Mix well and return to boil. Reduce heat to medium; cover tightly and cook 20 minutes, or until chicken is no longer pink and rice is tender.

To Freeze:
Cool. Place into labeled freezer bags; freeze.

To Serve:
Thaw. Place into large skillet; heat over medium heat until heated through. Serve.

Turkey Roll-Ups

6-8 servings

8 (thick) slices deli turkey-breast meat
1 package chicken Stove Top Stuffing Mix™
1 jar fat-free turkey gravy

Prepare stuffing according to package directions. Place a large tablespoon of stuffing in the middle of each turkey slice. Roll up and place, seam side down, in a freezable dish or on aluminum foil.

To Freeze:
Fold foil around the turkey roll-ups, label and freeze.

To Serve:
Preheat oven to 350 degrees. Place turkey roll-ups in a 9 x 12-inch baking dish, side by side. Pour gravy over roll-ups and cover with foil. Bake for 30 minutes or until heated through and bubbly. Serve with mashed potatoes and cranberry sauce.

Notes from the Chef...
A practically "instant" dinner. Use when rushed for time and make extras to freeze. Tastes great with mashed potatoes and cranberry sauce! Let kids roll up their sleeves and come up with other creative combos!

Braised Beef

6 servings

1 tablespoon olive oil
4 cups chopped onion
4 cups chopped carrots
1 garlic clove, minced
2 pounds lean boneless beef-
   roast

¼ teaspoon salt
1 cup dry red wine
1 bay leaf
1 teaspoon oregano
1 teaspoon thyme

Chop onion and carrots. Mince garlic. In Dutch oven, heat oil, add onions. Cook over medium-high heat stirring frequently until onions are golden brown. Add carrots and garlic. Cook until carrots are tender. Add roast to vegetable mixture; turning to brown on all sides. Stir in remaining ingredients; bring to boil. Reduce heat and simmer, covered, for 1½ hours (adding small amounts of water as needed to keep meat from sticking to pan). Remove beef from pan; slice.

To Freeze:
Cool. Place meat and vegetable mixture into labeled freezer bags. Freeze.

To Serve:
Thaw. Reheat in large skillet. Serve hot.

Beef Fajitas

6 servings

1 pound lean boneless beef, cut
   into ¼-inch strips
1 teaspoon cumin
1 teaspoon chili powder
½ teaspoon pepper
1 green bell pepper, seeded and
   sliced
1 cup sliced onion
¼ cup lime juice

For Serving Day:
12 (6-inch) flour tortillas
2 cups shredded lettuce
2 cups grated reduced-fat
   Cheddar cheese
1 cup salsa

Slice onion and green pepper. Cut raw meat into ¼-inch slices. Store in refrigerator until ready to use. Sprinkle beef on all sides with cumin, chili powder and black pepper. Spray large skillet with cooking spray. Heat. Add bell pepper and onion; cook over high heat stirring constantly until vegetables are lightly browned. Add beef, stirring constantly until beef is no longer pink. Add lime juice; toss to combine.

To Freeze:
Cool. Put into labeled freezer bag. Freeze.

To Serve:
Thaw completely. Reheat meat mixture in large skillet until heated through. Warm tortillas in microwave (if desired). To assemble fajitas, place an equal amount of warmed beef mixture onto center of each warmed tortilla. Top beef with ¼ cup lettuce, an equal amount of cheese and 2 tablespoons salsa. Roll tortillas to enclose filling and serve immediately.

Raspberry Pork Sirloin Roast

6-8 servings

2½-3 pound pork sirloin roast, boneless
2 teaspoons Lawry's Seasoning Salt™
1 teaspoon onion powder
1 teaspoon garlic powder
1 roasting bag

For Serving Day:
1 cup seedless raspberry jam, heated

Preheat oven to 325 degrees. Season the roast with the spices and place in the roasting bag. Place the roast in a small shallow roasting pan. Cook for 1 -1½ hours, or 25 minutes per pound. When internal temperature reaches 160 degrees the roast is cooked. Remove it from the oven and carefully pull from bag, using caution not to burn yourself. In a small microwave-safe bowl heat the 1 cup of jam for about 30-60 seconds.. Baste the roast with ¼ cup of the jam; serve the rest of the jam with the roast. Return basted roast to the oven for 10 more minutes. Cut the roast into ¼-½-inch thick medallions. Serve three to four medallions on a plate, one draped over the top of the others in a half-circle formation. Drizzle a line of warmed raspberry jam down the center of the medallions and serve.

To Freeze:
Wrap sliced medallions in foil and freeze. Do not cover with jam until serving day. Or wrap roast whole and slice at serving time.

To Serve:
To heat after freezing, thaw roast in the refrigerator overnight. Place the defrosted roast on a microwave safe plate and cook at 70 percent power for 8 to 15 minutes in the microwave (time depends on your microwave—check frequently). Slice and serve with reserved jam garnish as directed above.

Notes from the Chef...
Good side dishes to go with this main course are rice dishes of your choice. (My family particularly likes an herb and butter rice.) Mashed or baked potatoes are also good. Add rolls and a vegetable dish of your choice, and you have an elegant, not to mention nutritious meal.

Beef & Noodles

6 servings

1 pound lean boneless beef, cut
   into ¼-inch strips
2 medium onions, thinly sliced
2 cups small mushrooms, with
   ends removed
2 tablespoons margarine
2 tablespoons flour
1½ cups fat-free beef broth
1 teaspoon prepared mustard

½ teaspoon paprika
½ teaspoon salt
¼ teaspoon pepper
¼ cup fat-free sour cream

For Serving Day:
6 ounces wide egg noodles

Cut beef into ½-inch strips. Slice onions. Remove ends from mushrooms.
Store in refrigerator until ready to use. Spray large skillet with cooking
spray. Cook beef over medium-high heat until no longer pink, stirring
frequently. Remove from skillet. In same skillet, add onions, cooking until
golden brown. Add mushrooms, cooking until softened and lightly
browned. Remove vegetables from skillet. In same skillet, melt margarine;
sprinkle with flour to make a roux. Cook over medium-high heat until
bubbling, stirring constantly. While continuing to stir, add broth, mustard,
paprika, salt and pepper. Cook, stirring constantly until sauce is thickened.
Remove from heat. Stir in sour cream. Return beef, onions and mushrooms
to skillet and stir gently to coat.

To Freeze:
Pour into labeled freezer bags. Freeze.

To Serve:
Thaw completely. Warm meat mixture until heated through. Cook noodles.
Serve beef over hot cooked noodles.

Chicken and Pasta Primavera

6 servings

2-3 chicken breasts, cooked and chopped into bite-sized pieces
1 yellow onion, chopped
1-2 cloves fresh garlic
2-3 carrots, cleaned, peeled and cut diagonally
1 red bell pepper, cleaned and chopped into 1½-inch pieces
1 yellow squash, cleaned, sliced
½ pound fresh mushrooms, cleaned and sliced
½ pound fresh asparagus, broken into bite-sized pieces (when in season)
½ cup water
1-2 teaspoons chicken bouillon granules, or 2 bouillon cubes
3 tablespoons olive oil, divided

For Serving Day:
8 ounces of linguine noodles, cooked

Cook chicken breasts in pan sprayed with olive oil until no longer pink, without overcooking. Chop into bite-sized pieces and reserve. Sauté onion and fresh garlic in 1 tablespoon olive oil until onion becomes transparent. Add vegetables with remaining 2 tablespoons olive oil (harder veggies first, saving mushrooms and squash for last). Cook until tender-crisp, then add water and chicken bouillon. Simmer 4-5 minutes, avoiding overcooking or too-soft vegetables. Boil linguine noodles till 'al dente', about 7-8 minutes. Drain off liquid. Combine cooked chicken, cooked vegetables, cooked pasta and toss. Serve on a platter.

To Freeze:
Skip the simmer step of the vegetables; this will help prevent the vegetables becoming too soft during the reheating process. Do not add the squash or mushrooms until the day you plan to serve. Do not toss with linguini until serving day. Store cooled, cooked chicken and semi-cooked veggie mixture in plastic zip-lock bags in freezer until serving day.

To Serve:
Thaw chicken and vegetables overnight. Warm the mixture and add reserved squash and mushrooms; simmer 4-5 minutes till tender and heated through. Prepare linguini noodles according to package directions. Toss all and serve on platter as above.

Sherried Beef

6 servings

2 medium size sirloin tip steaks, cut up
2 packages dry onion soup mix
2 cans golden mushroom soup
1 cup cooking sherry
2 jars whole mushrooms, with juice
1 green pepper, chopped

Place all ingredients in a deep casserole dish. Cover and bake at 350 degrees for three hours.

To Freeze:
Transfer into freezer safe containers. Label and freeze.

To Serve:
Thaw in refrigerator over night. Bake in a 350 degree oven until heated through.

Dijon Pork Chops

6 servings

½ cup plain dried bread crumbs
3 tablespoons Parmesan cheese
3 tablespoons parsley
1 tablespoon vegetable oil
½ teaspoon pepper
6 pork chops
2 tablespoons Dijon mustard

In a pie plate, combine bread crumbs, Parmesan cheese, parsley, oil and pepper. Mix well. Set aside. Spread both sides of pork chops with mustard; press chops into bread crumb mixture, coating both sides. Spray rack in broiler pan with cooking spray; arrange chops on rack; broil 5-6 inches from element until cooked (5-6 minutes on each side). Remove from heat.

To Freeze:
Cool. Place chops in single layer onto cookie sheet; freeze. As soon as chops are frozen solid, remove from baking sheet and place frozen chops together in labeled freezer bag; return to freezer.

To Serve:
Thaw. Reheat chops in skillet over medium heat until heated through, turning once.

Stuffed Pork Chops

6 servings

6 thick-cut pork chops (about 1-inch thick; ask your butcher)
½ cup wild rice mix
2 tablespoons margarine or butter
2 cups sliced mushrooms
⅓ cup sherry
½ cup chopped onion
2 teaspoons pepper
1½ teaspoons paprika
1½ cups fat-free beef broth
2 tablespoons cornstarch

Chop onion. Slice mushrooms. Cook wild rice mixture according to package directions, substituting ⅓ cup sherry for ⅓ cup water in directions. Heat butter in skillet; add mushroom slices and onions and sauté until softened. Remove from heat. Stir ½ of the mushroom-onion mixture into the wild rice. Slice a pocket in each chop. Spoon 2-3 tablespoons of the wild rice mixture into each chop and secure with toothpicks. Rub pepper and paprika into chops. Broil chops on broiler rack 5-inches from the heat for 15 minutes (turning halfway through). Cool slightly. Remove toothpicks. For sauce, in saucepan stir together broth and cornstarch and cook until sauce begins to thicken. Add remaining sautéed mushrooms; cook and stir until sauce is thickened and bubbly, about 2 minutes more. Stir in 1 additional tablespoon sherry for flavor.

To Freeze:
Cool and place chops and sauce in large freezer bag; label and freeze.

To Serve:
Thaw. Place in 13 x 9 x 2-inch casserole dish. Bake in a 375-degree oven for 1 hour or until heated through. Spoon sauce over chops before serving.

Chicken Vegetable Skillet

6 servings

6 teaspoons olive oil or vegetable oil
1 pound potatoes, thinly sliced
1 pound boneless-chicken breasts, cut into 1-inch cubes
3 tablespoons butter or margarine
1 cup chopped onion
1 cup chopped green bell pepper
1 cup sliced carrot
3 garlic cloves, minced
1 (15 ounce) can Italian-style stewed tomatoes (with liquid)
3 tablespoons fresh parsley, chopped
½ teaspoon thyme
½ teaspoon salt
½ teaspoon pepper
1 teaspoon white vinegar or lemon juice

Cut chicken into 1-inch cubes. Chop onion and green pepper. Slice carrots. Mince garlic. Peel and thinly slice potatoes; place potatoes in a large bowl of cold water with 1 teaspoon white vinegar or lemon juice. Refrigerate potatoes until ready to use; dry thoroughly before adding to skillet. Chop stewed tomatoes, reserving liquid.

In large skillet, heat oil over medium-high heat; add (thoroughly dry) potatoes and chicken; cook until chicken is no longer pink, stirring constantly. Transfer mixture to another container and set aside. Using same skillet, melt butter and stir in onion, green pepper, carrot slices and garlic; cook over high heat until just barely tender. Add potato-chicken mixture to vegetables in skillet. Stir in tomatoes, tomato liquid and remaining spices. Reduce heat to low and cook, stirring frequently, until potatoes are just barely starting to get tender (less than 5 minutes).

To Freeze:
Remove from heat. Cool in refrigerator. Place mixture into labeled freezer bag; seal and freeze.

To Serve:
Thaw. Heat in large skillet over medium heat until heated through and potatoes are tender.

Chicken Pasta Italiano

6 servings

1 pound boneless-chicken breasts, cut into ½-inch strips
2 medium tomatoes, seeded and chopped
1 cup chopped onion
1 small zucchini, sliced
1 small red pepper, cut into thin strips
2 teaspoons olive oil
2 garlic cloves, minced
½ cup frozen peas
1 teaspoon salt
1 teaspoon dried Italian seasoning

For Serving Day:
6 ounces bow tie pasta, uncooked
½ cup Parmesan cheese

Seed and chop tomatoes. Chop onion. Slice zucchini. Cut red pepper into thin strips. Mince garlic. Cut chicken breasts into ½-inch strips.
In large skillet, heat oil over medium heat. Add garlic and chicken strips; cook 5 minutes, stirring frequently. Add onion, zucchini, red pepper, frozen peas, salt and Italian seasoning. Cook 1 minute longer. Remove from heat and stir in tomatoes.

To Freeze:
Cool. Place into labeled freezer bags. Freeze.

To Serve:
Thaw chicken mixture. Cook bow-tie pasta according to package directions. Drain. Heat chicken mixture in large skillet over medium heat until heated through. Toss together with cooked pasta; sprinkle with Parmesan cheese and serve immediately.

Ham and Cheese Casserole

6 servings

3 cups elbow macaroni, cooked
8 ounces Cheddar cheese, low-fat
8 ounces mozzarella cheese, part-skim milk
2 eggs
1½ cups skim milk
1 pound ham, cubed
1 teaspoon paprika

Combine eggs, milk and paprika in bowl. Layer ½ of noodles, ham and cheeses in baking dish. Repeat. Pour egg-milk mixture over top.

To Freeze:
Store in freezer-safe containers, label and freeze.

To Serve:
Thaw overnight and bake for 30-45 minutes in a 375-degree oven, or until no longer runny (will be slightly soft). Let set for 5 minutes before serving.

Beef & Brown Rice

6 servings

1 pound ground round
1½ cups brown rice
1 (8 ounce) bag frozen green peas
1 can spicy Rotel™ brand tomatoes
1 large onion, chopped
2 tablespoons butter
2 cups shredded Monterey Jack cheese
Mrs. Dash™ *or* Grill Mates™ *or* pepper, salt, & garlic, to taste
1 cup mushrooms (optional)

Sauté meat, onions and mushrooms in 2 tablespoons butter. Cook brown rice for 10 minutes in boiling water. Drain rice. Combine all ingredients in freezer/oven safe container. Season to your liking.

To Freeze:
Cool, cover, label and freeze.

To Serve:
Thaw overnight. Cook at 350 degrees for 30-40 minutes or until heated through.

Notes from the Chef...

This is a wonderful one-dish meal and can be customized to your taste preferences. We use this as a base recipe and have made some great creations. The brown rice gives the meal a more satisfying texture and is healthier too.

Easy Chicken Enchiladas

6 servings

1 pound chicken breasts
juice of one lime
1 clove garlic, crushed
¼ cup chopped onion
1 tablespoon chopped-fresh cilantro, optional
1 can cream of chicken soup
8 ounces sour cream
1 cup taco sauce
2 cups grated mozzarella cheese
1 cup grated Cheddar cheese, (to mix in with the mozzarella)
10-12 flour tortillas
1 cup sliced black olives, divided

Simmer chicken with crushed garlic, cilantro, onion and lime juice until cooked. Drain and shred chicken. In medium bowl mix together soup and sour cream. Reserve ½ of soup mixture for later. Stir in shredded chicken, taco sauce, ½ cup olives and 1 cup mixed cheeses. Roll about ½ cup chicken filling into each tortilla. No need to fold edges, just roll. Place in lightly greased 9 X 13-inch baking dish. Cover tortillas with remaining soup mixture, especially the edges. Top with remaining olives and cheese. Cover with foil. Bake at 350 degrees for 20-25 minutes. Remove foil the last 5 minutes.

To Freeze:
Assemble as above but prior to baking cover uncooked meal with foil. Label, date and freeze.

To Serve:
Thaw for a few hours. No need to thaw completely. Bake 30-35 minutes in a 350-degree oven or until heated through. Remove foil the last 5 minutes as above.

Italian Sausage and Squash in a Skillet

6 servings

1¼ pounds uncooked Italian sausage (use mild or spicy)
3 small, yellow squash or zucchini (cubed)
½ cup chopped onion
1 (14.5 ounce) can stewed tomatoes (Rotel™ tomatoes give a spicier flavor)
2 green onions, tops only, chopped
3 cups hot cooked rice (brown or white)

Brown sausage over medium heat until no longer pink. Drain off fat and slice sausage into ¼-inch pieces. Return sausage to pan and cook until golden brown. Add squash and onions; cook and stir for 2-3 minutes. Stir in tomatoes. Reduce heat; cover and simmer for 15 minutes or until squash is tender. While meal is simmering, prepare rice according to package directions. Serve over hot rice.

To Freeze:
Skip preparing the rice and keep it on hand for serving day. Cool meal and place into freezer-safe containers.

To Serve:
Thaw for a few hours and then warm over medium heat. While heating, prepare rice according to package directions. Serve over hot rice.

Label Your Pantry Too!

It's a good idea to clearly label the ingredients that you need for serving day which are kept in your cupboards or pantry. There is nothing worse than planning a meal only to find you are now missing the ingredients for its completion!

Chicken Cordon Blue

6 servings

6 boneless, skinless chicken breasts
6 thin slices of good ham
½ pound Swiss cheese, cut into 6 strips
6 ounces cream cheese, cut into 6 strips
2 eggs
2 cups herbed bread crumbs
3 tablespoons Parmesan cheese

Pound chicken breasts till about ⅛-inch thick (or as thin as you can without tearing the meat). Center a slice of ham on each pounded-chicken fillet, (ham slice should be slightly smaller than chicken—trim if necessary). Place a strip of Swiss cheese and a strip of cream cheese on bottom edge of chicken and tightly roll chicken, folding in sides. Carefully make sure all of the ham and cheeses are covered. Beat eggs. Coat all sides of chicken-rolls generously with egg by rolling each in beaten egg. Mix bread crumbs with parmesan cheese. Roll chicken in bread crumbs. Place on cookie sheet and bake at 350 degrees for 45-50 minutes or until chicken is thoroughly cooked and juices run clear. Some cheese may melt out.

To Freeze:
Do not bake. Place un-cooked chicken rolls on cookie sheet and cover with plastic wrap. Freeze till mostly firm and then transfer individual breasts into freezer-safe bags.

To Serve:
Thaw for several hours. Follow baking instructions above, increasing cooking time 5-10 minutes, if necessary.

Home-style Lasagna

6-8 servings

1 pound ground beef
1 pound sausage (any kind)
1 box lasagna noodles
2 (15 ounce) cans tomato sauce
2 (8 ounce) bags of shredded mozzarella cheese
1 (8 ounce) container of cottage cheese
4 tablespoons Italian seasoning
1 small onion, diced
salt and pepper to taste

Brown ground beef, sausage and onion. Drain. Add tomato sauce, Italian seasoning, salt and pepper. Cook 10 minutes or until bubbly. In separate pot boil lasagna noodles according to package directions. Drain and rinse under cold water to keep from sticking together. Spray a 9 x 13-inch pan (use an aluminum disposable pan if freezing for longer than a week). Layer noodles, meat sauce, cottage cheese and mozzarella cheese. Repeat to the top of pan. Cover tightly to keep fresh.

To Freeze:
Cover, label and freeze.

To Serve:
When ready to cook, either thaw to room temperature and bake at 350 degrees for 30 minutes or if frozen 350 degrees about 45 to 50 minutes, or until cheese is bubbly and slightly browned on top. Serve with side salad and garlic bread for complete meal; or serve alone as this is zesty and filling.

Magnificent Mac

6 servings

3 cups chicken broth
1½ cups skim milk
¾ pound elbow macaroni
1½ tablespoons cornstarch
1½ cups frozen peas
½ pound Canadian bacon, cubed
8 ounces Cheddar cheese, shredded

In a large sauce pan or Dutch oven bring broth, milk and macaroni to a boil. Cook for 10 minutes, stirring frequently. Blend cornstarch with 5 tablespoons of water. Stir into pan and continue cooking and stirring until mixture returns to a boil. Add peas and Canadian bacon; mix well and then remove from heat. Add cheese and stir for 1-2 more minutes to combine.

To Freeze:
Transfer to freezer-safe containers. Cool, label and freeze.

To Serve:
Thaw to room temperature and warm over medium heat until heated through. Serve with warm French bread and a tossed salad for a complete meal.

Susie's Sloppy Joes

5-7 servings

1 pound ground beef
½ cup chopped onion
½ cup chopped celery
½ cup chopped green pepper
½ cup water
½ cup catsup
2 teaspoons Worcestershire sauce
1½ teaspoon brown sugar
1 teaspoon vinegar
½ teaspoon lemon juice
Salt and pepper to taste

For serving day:
Hamburger buns

Brown beef in a Dutch oven over medium heat and drain fat. Add remaining ingredients; mix well. Simmer on low heat for 2 hours.

To Freeze:
Cool and transfer into freezer safe containers. Label and freeze.

To Serve:
Thaw in refrigerator over night. Warm on stovetop until heated through. Serve on hamburger buns.

Baked Ziti

18 servings

This is one of those recipes my family never seems to eat often enough. Everyone loves it, even my three-year-old. "More yummy noodles, Mommy!"

3 pounds ziti (or penne) pasta
1 pound ground beef (optional)
1 cup chopped onion
1 cup chopped green pepper
2 jars commercial spaghetti sauce (or 6 cups homemade)

For Serving Day:
3 cups grated mozzarella cheese, divided
¾ cup grated parmesan cheese, divided

Cook pasta until just barely tender; drain thoroughly and rinse with cold water to stop cooking process. Brown ground beef; drain off fat. Add onion and green pepper to meat and sauté until vegetables are softened. (If needed, add small amount of olive oil during sauté process.) Add spaghetti sauce and mix well. Combine completed sauce and cooked pasta, mixing well.

To Freeze:
Divide into 3 (gallon-size) freezer bags; label. Divide grated mozzarella cheese into 3 (quart-size) freezer bags and attach to pasta bags. Label and freeze, along with final cooking instructions.

To Serve:
Thaw. Spread pasta into 9 x 13-inch baking pan. Sprinkle 1 cup mozzarella cheese evenly over pasta. Sprinkle ¼ cup parmesan cheese over top. Cover dish and bake for 30 minutes at 350 degrees, or until bubbly on the edges and hot in the middle. Remove foil and bake uncovered for five more minutes.

Chicken and Broccoli

16 servings

1 cup margarine
1 cup flour
8 cups milk
salt and pepper to taste
4 cups chopped-cooked chicken, divided
2 pounds broccoli, steamed and divided
2 pounds Cheddar cheese, grated and divided

To make white sauce, melt margarine in a large heavy pan. Add flour, stirring constantly. When mixture reaches the boiling point, add milk, mixing constantly with a wire whisk. Heat until almost boiling, stirring constantly. Remove from heat. Place cooked chicken into 4 (8 x 8-inch) baking pans. Divide steamed broccoli and place over chicken. Pour white sauce over all. Sprinkle each pan with grated cheese.

To Freeze:
Cover pans with foil; label and freeze. This recipe can also be frozen in zip-top freezer bags to conserve space in your freezer. If storing in bags, divide grated cheese among smaller freezer bags and freeze separately from the chicken and broccoli mixture.

To Serve:
Thaw. Bake at 350 degrees for 30 minutes. Serve over cooked rice or spaghetti noodles for a Tetrazzini-type meal.

Easy Baked Pasta

6 servings

1 cup mozzarella cheese
2 tablespoons olive oil
2 pounds ground beef
3 cloves crushed garlic
1 cup spaghetti sauce
¾ cup brown gravy
1 cup milk
1 teaspoon oregano
½ teaspoon rosemary
1 pound mostaccioli noodles
1 (4 ounce) can mushrooms, drained

Brown beef and garlic over medium heat. Drain fat. Add all remaining ingredients, except cheese and pasta and mix well. Prepare pasta according to package direction in a separate pot, undercook several minutes if freezing this dish. Drain pasta and mix with sauce. Pour into a 9 x 13 inch casserole dish or aluminum pan (if freezing.) Top with mozzarella cheese. Bake, uncovered, at 350 degrees for 25 minutes.

To Freeze:
Transfer into freezer safe containers. Label and freeze.

To Serve:
Thaw in refrigerator over night. Cook in a 350-degree oven until heated through.

Old Fashioned Beef Stew

6 servings

1 tablespoon olive oil
1½ cups chopped onion
2 garlic cloves, minced
3 teaspoons flour
1 teaspoon salt
½ teaspoon pepper
1 pound lean boneless beef, cut into 2-inch cubes
1 pound small red potatoes, quartered
1 cup small white mushrooms, ends removed
1½ cups pearl onions
1½ cups baby carrots
3 cups reduced-fat beef broth
½ cup red wine vinegar
2 tablespoons tomato paste
½ teaspoon thyme
½ teaspoon tarragon
2 bay leaves
2 tablespoons parsley

Chop first onions listed. Mince garlic. Cut beef into 2-inch cubes. Cut small red potatoes into quarters; store in large pan of water in refrigerator until ready to use. In large skillet, cook onions and garlic in olive oil until softened. On a plate, combine flour, ½ the salt and ½ the pepper. Dredge beef with flour mixture to coat evenly. Add beef to onions and garlic and cook stirring frequently, until beef is browned on all sides. Add mushrooms, pearl onions and carrots; cook stirring frequently for 2 minutes. Add broth, vinegar, tomato paste, thyme, tarragon, bay leaves, remaining salt and pepper, and 5 cups water. Bring to boil. Reduce heat to low and simmer covered 20 minutes. Drain and add the potatoes. Cook an additional 5 minutes (potatoes will still be firm). Remove from heat.

To Freeze:
Cool quickly. Freeze in labeled freezer bags.

To Serve:
Thaw. Heat over medium heat until heated through. Discard bay leaves, stir in parsley. Serve hot.

CHAPTER SEVEN

Vegetarian

Vegetable Fried Rice

6 servings

1½ cups long grain rice
4 eggs, beaten
½ cup sliced green onions
½ cup minced fresh cilantro
2 tablespoons soy sauce
½ teaspoon sugar
1 tablespoon oriental sesame oil
1½ cups washed leeks, cut into thin strips
1½ 2 cups thinly sliced carrots
1½ cups diced red bell pepper
3 tablespoons grated fresh ginger root
6 garlic cloves, minced
½ cup coarsely chopped, unsalted peanuts
3 tablespoons cider vinegar
½ teaspoon salt

Cook rice according to package directions. Slice green onions, leeks and carrots. Chop bell pepper. Grate fresh ginger root. Mince garlic. Chop peanuts. In bowl, combine eggs, ½ of the green onions, sugar, ½ of the cilantro, ½ of the soy sauce and 2 tablespoons water. Spray large skillet with cooking spray. Over medium-high heat, scramble egg mixture until no longer wet. In another large skillet, heat sesame oil over medium-high heat; sauté leeks, carrots and bell pepper until softened. Remove from heat. Add ginger and garlic. Stir to combine. Add rice, peanuts, vinegar, salt, egg mixture, remaining green onions, cilantro and soy sauce. Mix well.

To Freeze:
Place into large labeled freezer bag; seal and freeze.

To Serve:
Thaw. Reheat in large skillet over medium-high heat until heated through. Add a small amount of sesame oil while warming if too dry.

Ricotta Broccoli Pie

6 servings

1 cup reduced-fat ricotta cheese
1 cup skim milk
3 eggs
¼ cup grated Parmesan cheese
½ teaspoon orange zest (finely grated orange part of orange peel)
2 teaspoons olive oil
3 garlic cloves, minced
1 (10 ounce) package frozen chopped broccoli, thawed and drained
1 tablespoon basil

Grate orange peel to make ½ teaspoon zest. Mince garlic. In blender or food processor, combine ricotta cheese, milk and eggs. Blend until smooth. Add Parmesan cheese and orange zest. Process until combined. In large skillet, sauté garlic in olive oil; add broccoli and basil; cook 2 minutes. In large bowl, combine ricotta mixture and broccoli.

To Freeze:
Pour into labeled freezer bag; seal and freeze.

To Serve:
Thaw. Squish bag gently to re-combine. Spray 9-inch pie plate with cooking spray. Pour mixture into pie plate. Bake in 350-degree oven for 40 minutes or until lightly browned and set. Let set 10 minutes before slicing into wedges.

Cheese & Veggie Quesadillas

6 servings

12 flour tortillas
4 cups grated reduced-fat Monterey Jack cheese
1 cup frozen broccoli pieces (or fresh)
1 (6 ounce) can black beans, drained and rinsed
1 tablespoon lime juice
¼ cup canned green chilies
¼ cup chopped fresh cilantro
¼ cup sliced green onions

For Serving Day:
1 cup salsa (mild or medium, according to taste)
3 tablespoons fat-free sour cream

Grate cheese. Drain and rinse canned black beans. Cook broccoli until just tender. In small bowl, mash beans and lime juice to form a paste. Stir in chilies, cilantro and green onions.

To Freeze:
Place into labeled freezer bag. Place cooked broccoli into small freezer bag. In large labeled freezer bag, put the bag of bean mixture, the bag of cooked broccoli and the bag of tortillas. Seal, freeze, label and date, along with finishing instructions.

To Serve:
Thaw. Spray two cookie sheets with cooking spray. Place 6 tortillas, in a single layer, onto cookie sheets. Spread bean mixture, evenly divided, between tortillas. Spread almost to edge of tortilla. Sprinkle broccoli pieces onto bean mixture. Top each tortilla with remaining tortillas. On two oven racks, bake in 450-degree oven until tortillas are lightly browned. Halfway through baking time switch cookie sheets on racks in the oven. Slide quesadillas onto cutting board; cut each into 6 wedges. Serve with cold salsa and dollops of sour cream.

Three Cheese Lasagna

6 servings

1 pound green spinach lasagna noodles
½ cup margarine
6 tablespoons flour
4 cups skim milk
¼ cup grated Parmesan cheese
½ cup grated Gruyere cheese
½ cup grated reduced-fat mozzarella
¼ teaspoon salt
⅛ teaspoon pepper
dash nutmeg

For Serving Day:
additional grated Parmesan cheese

Prepare green lasagna noodles according to package directions. Rinse in cold water. In large saucepan, melt the margarine over low heat. Stir in the flour, making a roux. Heat for 1 minute. Gradually stir in the milk, stirring constantly until thickened. Add the cheeses, salt, pepper and nutmeg to sauce; stir until cheeses melt. Spray a deep casserole dish with generous amount of cooking spray. Add alternating layers of lasagna noodles and sauce. Finish with a layer of sauce.

To Freeze:
Wrap with foil; label and freeze.

To Serve:
Thaw. Uncover and sprinkle with a light dusting of Parmesan cheese. Bake in 350-degree oven for 45 minutes, or until heated through, bubbling and golden brown.

Baked Spaghetti

6 servings

12 ounces spaghetti noodles, cooked
3 (14 ounce) cans diced tomatoes
1½ cups chopped onion
2 teaspoons Italian seasoning
1 cup grated reduced-fat Cheddar cheese
3 tablespoons grated Parmesan cheese

Cook spaghetti noodles according to package directions until just barely tender; or slightly undercooked to avoid mushy noodles when freezing and reheating. Chop onions. Grate cheese. Spray 9 x 13-inch baking dish with cooking spray. Place spaghetti in bottom of pan. Pour tomatoes over the noodles. Add onion; sprinkle with Italian seasoning. Sprinkle the Cheddar cheese over the top of the spaghetti mixture; top with Parmesan cheese.

To Freeze:
Cover with foil; label and freeze.

To Serve:
Thaw. Bake in 350-degree oven for 30-35 minutes, or until hot and bubbly.

Presto Mac

6 servings

1 pound dried elbow macaroni
⅓ cup butter or margarine, melted
2 cups shredded Cheddar cheese, divided
½ cup bread crumbs, divided
3 large eggs
2 cups milk
¼ teaspoon pepper
¼ teaspoon salt

Cook macaroni just until tender. Drain. Return macaroni to pan. Remove from heat. Add butter (or margarine) and ¾ cup cheese and stir to mix. Spray a casserole dish with cooking spray. Sprinkle some cheese and ½ of the bread crumbs on the bottom of the casserole dish. In a bowl, combine eggs, milk, salt and pepper. Add this mixture to macaroni and stir well. If serving immediately, continue with recipe topping found in "to serve" instructions.

To Freeze:
Transfer mixture to prepared-casserole dish or disposable aluminum pan. Wrap pan tightly with additional foil. Place remaining cheese and breadcrumbs in freezer-bags and tape to aluminum pan, along with label, date and instructions for finishing the dish.

To Serve:
Thaw to room temperature. Top with remaining cheese and breadcrumbs. Bake in a 400-degree oven for 20-30 minutes or until heated through and bubbly.

Eggplant Bake

6 servings

2 medium-sized eggplants, cut into ¼-inch thick slices
2½ teaspoons salt
⅔ cup malt vinegar
2½ tablespoons vegetable oil
2 large onions, peeled and sliced into rings
1 (4 ounce) can green chilies
1 (16 ounce) can stewed tomatoes, cut up and drained
¾ teaspoon chili powder
1 garlic clove, minced
¾ teaspoon ground turmeric
8 tomatoes, sliced
1½ cups nonfat plain yogurt
1¼ teaspoons ground black pepper
1 cup grated reduced-fat Cheddar cheese

Slice eggplant into ¼-inch thick slices. Slice onions into rings. Slice tomatoes. Grate cheese. Arrange the eggplant slices in a shallow baking dish and sprinkle with 1½ teaspoons of the salt. Pour the malt vinegar over the top, cover and marinate 30 minutes. Drain eggplant well; discard marinade liquid. In large skillet, heat the vegetable oil and gently sauté onion rings until golden brown. Add chilies, remaining teaspoon of salt, chopped stewed tomatoes, chili powder, garlic and turmeric. Mix well; simmer for 5 minutes. Remove sauce from heat and cool slightly. In blender or food processor, blend to a smooth purée. Arrange ½ the eggplant slices in base of shallow ovenproof dish sprayed with cooking spray. Spoon ½ the tomato sauce over eggplant slices; cover with remaining eggplant; top with remaining tomato sauce and sliced tomatoes. In small bowl, combine yogurt, black pepper and Cheddar cheese. Pour over tomato slices. Bake in 350-degree oven for 20 minutes.

To Freeze:
Remove from oven; cool. Wrap with foil; label and freeze.

To Serve:
Thaw. Bake in 375-degree oven for 15 minutes or until heated through and topping is golden brown. Serve hot straight from the oven.

Italian Garden Pasta

6 servings

1 (10 ounce) package frozen spinach, thawed and well drained
3 tablespoons olive oil
1 pound mushrooms, sliced
1 medium onion, chopped
1 (16 ounce) can Italian-style stewed
tomatoes, cut up into small pieces, in liquid

For Serving Day
1 pound dried macaroni
¼ cup Parmesan cheese

Slice mushrooms. Chop onion. Thaw spinach.
Drain well. Pat with dry paper towels to
remove as much liquid as possible. In large
saucepan, heat olive oil. Add mushrooms and
onions; cook until vegetables are softened. Remove from heat. Stir in
Italian-style stewed tomatoes (and the tomato liquid). Add spinach. Stir
until combined.

> **Minimize Your Tears**
> When chopping onions, chop as many as you can stand. Freeze them in ½ cup portions to use in future recipes. Onions keep well for several months in the freezer.

To Freeze:
Place in labeled freezer bag; freeze.

To Serve:
Thaw sauce. Cook pasta according to package directions. Heat sauce in
large skillet just until heated through. Toss pasta with sauce. Sprinkle with
Parmesan cheese.

Spaghetti Pie

6 servings

6 ounces dry spaghetti noodles
2 tablespoons margarine
½ cup parmesan cheese
2 eggs, beaten
1 teaspoon vegetable oil
½ cup onion, chopped
1 (16 ounce) can Italian-style stewed tomatoes, with liquid
1 (6 ounce) can tomato paste
1 teaspoon sugar
1 teaspoon oregano
½ clove garlic, minced
1 cup fat-free cottage cheese
4 ounces reduced-fat Cheddar cheese, grated (or mozzarella, or Monterey Jack)

Chop onion. Mince garlic. Cook spaghetti noodles according to package directions. Drain. Stir margarine into hot noodles until melted. Stir in Parmesan cheese and beaten eggs. Spray 9-inch pie plate with cooking spray. Form pasta mixture into a crust-shape in bottom and up sides of pie plate. Store covered in refrigerator until ready to use. In a skillet, heat vegetable oil. Cook onion until softened. Add tomatoes, tomato paste, sugar, oregano and garlic. Heat through. Spread cottage cheese over bottom of spaghetti crust. Top with tomato mixture. Sprinkle grated cheese over all.

To Freeze:
Cover pie with foil; label and freeze.

To Serve:
Thaw. Bake covered for 25 minutes at 350 degrees. Remove foil and bake for 5 more minutes or until cheese is lightly browned.

Cheese Manicotti

6 servings

½ cup chopped onion
1 clove garlic, minced
1 tablespoon vegetable oil
1 (16 ounce) can Italian-style stewed tomatoes, cut up
1 (8 ounce) can tomato sauce
⅓ cup water
1 teaspoon sugar
1 teaspoon oregano
1 teaspoon thyme
¼ teaspoon salt
1 bay leaf
12 manicotti shells
2 eggs, beaten
1½ cups fat-free cottage cheese
8 ounces (2 cups) reduced-fat mozzarella cheese, grated
¼ cup grated Parmesan cheese
¼ cup chopped parsley
dash pepper

Chop onion. Mince garlic. Grate mozzarella cheese. Cook manicotti shells according to package directions. Rinse in cold water. Store in large pan of cold water until ready to use. In large saucepan, heat salad oil; add onion and garlic; cook until onion is softened. Stir in tomatoes, tomato sauce, water, sugar, oregano, thyme, salt and bay leaf. Bring to boil. Simmer uncovered, for 45 minutes. In mixing bowl, combine eggs, cottage cheese, mozzarella cheese, Parmesan cheese, parsley and pepper. Drain manicotti shells. Spoon cheese mixture into manicotti. Pour half of tomato mixture into 13 x 9-inch baking dish. Place stuffed shells into pan; pour remaining sauce over top of shells.

To Freeze:
Cover with foil. Label and freeze.

To Serve:
Thaw. Bake, covered, in 350-degree oven for 45 minutes or until hot and bubbly.

Mexican Noodle Bake

6 servings

2 tablespoons vegetable oil
1 cup chopped onion
1 cup chopped green pepper
1 cup sliced celery
1 package taco seasoning
1 (15 ounce) can black beans, drained and rinsed
1 (15 ounce) can red kidney beans, un-drained
1 (16 ounce) can tomato sauce
1 (16 ounce) can diced tomatoes
2 cups elbow macaroni, dry

For Serving Day:
1 cup grated reduced-fat Cheddar cheese

Chop onion and green pepper. Slice celery. Cook macaroni according to package directions. Drain and rinse in cold water. Grate cheese.
In large skillet, sauté onion, green pepper and celery in hot oil until softened. Stir in taco seasoning, black beans, kidney beans, tomato sauce and diced tomatoes. Simmer for 10 minutes. Remove from heat. Stir in cooked noodles. Spread bean and noodle mixture into 9x13-inch casserole dish. Bake uncovered in a 375-degree oven until heated through, about 25-30 minutes.

To Freeze:
Wrap with foil; label and freeze. Place grated cheese in small freezer bag; attach to casserole dish. Label and include final cooking instructions.

To Serve:
Thaw. Sprinkle grated cheese over top of casserole. Bake uncovered in 375-degree oven for 45 minutes or until center is hot and edges are bubbly.

Colored Containers
Consider using colored containers to help store your food. You may want to color-code and separate by main ingredients (beef, pork, etc.) or by meal-type (breakfast, lunch, or dinner.)

Spinach Pie

6 servings

1 (16 ounce) loaf frozen bread dough, thawed
2 (10 ounce) packages frozen chopped spinach
½ cup chopped onion
1 garlic clove, minced
1 tablespoon olive oil
1 beaten egg
1 (15 ounce) carton reduced-fat ricotta cheese
½ cup grated Parmesan cheese
1 (8 ounce) jar pizza sauce

For Serving Day:
2 cups grated reduced-fat mozzarella cheese

Let frozen bread dough rise according to package directions; punch down. Cover; let rest 5 minutes before using for pie. Chop onion. Grate mozzarella cheese. Cook spinach according to package directions; drain well and pat dry. Line 9 x 13-inch casserole dish with heavy foil. Spray foil lining thoroughly with cooking spray. Using rolling pin, roll dough into approximately a 14 x 10-inch rectangle. Place into foil-lined baking dish, patting onto bottom and up sides. Prick bottom and sides of dough with fork. Bake dough crust in a 425-degree oven for 10 minutes or until dough starts to brown. Remove from oven; cool. In a small skillet, sauté onion and garlic in olive oil until softened; remove from heat. In medium bowl, combine egg, ricotta, Parmesan cheese, spinach and onion mixture. Spread over crust. Pour pizza sauce over all. Bake in a 375-degree oven for 20 minutes. Top with mozarella cheese and bake 10 minutes more.

To Freeze:
Stop preparation just after pouring pizza sauce. Freeze for 2 hours or until firm. Lift pie with foil out of pan. Seal with more foil; label and freeze. Place grated mozzarella in small freezer bag; label, seal and attach to main package, with final cooking instructions.

To Serve:
No need to thaw. Place frozen spinach pie on baking sheet. Remove top foil. Bake in a 375-degree oven for one hour or until heated through. Top with mozzarella cheese. Bake about 10 minutes more or till cheese melts. Let stand 5 minutes; remove foil. Note: If thawed first, bake in a 375-degree oven for 20 minutes. Top with cheese. Bake 10 minutes more. Let stand 5 minutes before serving.

CHAPTER EIGHT

Desserts

Melts In Your Mouth Pie

8 servings

1 box graham crackers
2 packages (4-serving size) vanilla instant pudding
4 cups ice cold milk
1 (8 ounce) tub of Cool Whip™
1 can of chocolate frosting

Mix the pudding according to package directions and stir the Cool Whip™ into the pudding. In a 9 x 13-inch pan, place a layer of graham crackers on the bottom of the pan, then spread ½ of the pudding mixture over the graham crackers and repeat the layers. Place one more layer of the graham crackers over the top of the pudding mixture. Remove the foil cover from the can of frosting and place the lid loosely over the top of the frosting. Place in the microwave for 1 minute. The frosting should be melted and runny. Pour the frosting over the top of the graham crackers and spread it out evenly. Refrigerate for several hours or overnight and serve cold.

To Freeze:
Transfer cooled slices into freezer-safe containers.

To Serve:
Transfer to refrigerator to thaw. Serve cold.

Mom's Texas
Fudge Sheet Cake

24 servings

Cake:
2 cups flour
2 cups sugar
2 sticks margarine
4 tablespoons cocoa
2 eggs (or equivalent in Egg-Beaters™)
½ cup sour milk
1 teaspoon baking soda
1 teaspoon cinnamon
1 teaspoon vanilla

Icing:
1 stick margarine
4 tablespoons cocoa
½ cup milk
1 box confectioners' sugar
1 teaspoon vanilla
1 teaspoon cinnamon
1 cup chopped nuts

Preheat oven to 375 degrees. Put flour and sugar in large mixing bowl. Bring margarine, cocoa and 1 cup water to a boil on the stovetop. Pour hot cocoa mixture over flour-sugar mixture and beat well. Add eggs, milk, baking soda, cinnamon and vanilla; beat until smooth. Pour into greased 11 x 14-inch baking sheet. Bake for 20 minutes at 375 degrees. Prepare icing by bringing margarine, cocoa and milk to a boil on the stovetop. Remove and beat in sugar, vanilla, nuts and cinnamon. Spread on warm cake. Let cool and cut into 1 or 2-inch squares.

To Freeze:
Transfer cooled cake to freezer-safe containers and freeze.

To Serve:
Let thaw at room temperature before serving. Great for unexpected company!

Easy Apple Pie

6 servings

6 cups peeled and sliced apples
¾ cup firmly packed brown sugar
4 tablespoons all-purpose flour
2 teaspoons ground cinnamon
½ teaspoon ground nutmeg

For serving day:
2 (9-inch) pie shells

Stir first five ingredients together until well-mixed. Place mixture in a foil pie plate.

To Freeze:
Wrap filling with heavy foil. Date, label and freeze for up to four months.

To Serve:
Preheat oven to 375 degrees. Pop filling out and transfer into a 9-inch pie shell. Top with second shell and flute edges. Pierce vent holes in top of pie. Bake for 45 minutes or until filling is warm and bubbly.

Notes from the Chef:
You can also make this pie with any other fruit or berries. If you choose to try berries, use granulated sugar in place of brown sugar.

Frozen Cranberry Mold

6-8 servings

1 can jellied cranberry sauce
2 tablespoons lemon juice
1 pint whipping cream
¼ cup mayonnaise
¼ cup powdered sugar
mint sprigs, optional

Blend cranberry sauce and lemon juice and pour into the bottom of a mold. Freeze. Whip the heavy cream, mayonnaise and powdered sugar together until thickened and soft peaks begin to form. (Use a chilled bowl to aid whipping.) Pour the whipped mixture over the freezing cranberry layer. Return to freezer until mold is completely frozen and set.

To Freeze:
If storing for a period of time make sure to wrap tightly with foil. Not recommended for long-term storage, 2-3 weeks maximum like homemade ice cream.

To Serve:
Pull from freezer about 20 minutes before serving. Unmold onto serving dish and garnish with sprigs of mint (optional). Serve slightly thawed.

Notes from the Chef:
To unmold easily, invert mold onto a plate. Wrap mold with a hot towel to warm the surface, until the dessert releases from the side of the mold and slides onto the plate. This cranberry mold also makes a nice side dish, in place of a salad, with pork or turkey.

Any-Berry Sauce

4 cups fresh berries (raspberries, blackberries, blueberries, strawberries)
½ cup granulated sugar

Combine ingredients in a saucepan over low heat until well-blended. If you like a thicker sauce, add up to 2 tablespoons of cornstarch. If using a seeded fruit, force sauce through a fine mesh sieve to remove seeds, then cool. Freeze for up to 6 months.

To Serve:
Simply leave sauce in refrigerator overnight.

Notes from the Chef:
This is a great recipe to preserve fresh berries!

Super Heath™ Bar Sandwich

12 servings

2 packages brownie mix
1 cup crumbled Heath™ bar, (or substitute chocolate chips)
4 cups vanilla ice cream, softened
additional ½ cup crumbled Heath™ bar (or chocolate chips)

For Serving Day:
Hot fudge or chocolate sauce

Prepare brownies according to directions, adding the 1 cup of crumbled Heath™ bar (or chocolate chips) to batter. Bake and cool completely. Freeze brownie layers until easy to handle, at least two hours. Spread ice cream over first layer, top with additional ½ cup Heath™ bar crumbles and cover with second brownie layer. Wrap in plastic-wrap and freeze until set.

Mark It!
Keep a roll of masking tape and a Sharpie™ marker in an assessable drawer for quick and easy labeling.

To Freeze:
Slice into desired serving size and freeze in freezer-safe containers for up to 6 weeks or freeze whole and slice at time of serving.

To Serve:
Remove from freezer and let sit 15 minutes before cutting into wedges or squares. Warm hot fudge (or chocolate) sauce and drizzle over wedges. Serve.

Wendy's Rum Raisin Ice Cream

1 quart French Vanilla ice cream (quality brand)
1 cup white raisins
½ cup light rum

Plump raisins in rum overnight. Drain off any excess rum and discard. Set raisins aside. Soften the ice cream just enough to easily fold in raisins—be careful not to thaw ice cream too much. Return ice cream to freezer to re-harden. Stores as you would any ice cream.

Notes from the Chef:
Serve as a simple, elegant dessert after a rich meal.

Strawberry Yogurt Pie

6-8 servings

1 (8-ounce) package cream cheese, softened
⅔ cup plain yogurt
⅓ cup nonfat dry milk powder
⅓ cup honey
1 (8-inch) graham cracker crust

For Serving Day:
2 cups sliced fresh strawberries
Strawberry sauce (optional see page XX)

Beat first four ingredients in a mixing bowl and spoon into crust.

To Freeze:
Wrap securely with foil and freeze for up to one month.

To Serve:
Thaw for 30 minutes. Slice fresh strawberries and top pie. Top with strawberry sauce, if desired.

Cookies & Cream Pie

6-8 servings

7 cups Cookies and Cream ice cream, slightly softened
1 (9-inch) chocolate crumb crust
1 Hershey™ bar

Spoon softened ice cream into crust. Melt Hershey™ bar in microwave until smooth. Drizzle over pie and freeze for 6-8 hours.

To Freeze:
Cut pie into slices or leave whole, whichever your preference. Wrap securely with foil and freeze.

To Serve:
Let stand 15 minutes before slicing and serving. Keeps in freezer for up to 2 months.

Chocolate Mocha Pie

6-8 servings

3 cups chocolate ice cream, softened
⅓ cup strong-brewed coffee, cooled
1 (3 ounce) package cream cheese, softened
½ cup chocolate syrup
2 tablespoons sugar
1 cup whipped topping
1 (9-inch) graham cracker crust

For Serving Day:
1 Heath™ candy bar, crushed

In a large mixing bowl, beat ice cream and coffee until well-blended. In a small mixing bowl, beat cream cheese, chocolate syrup and sugar. Fold in whipped topping. Combine chocolate mixture and ice cream mixture; then pour into crust and freeze until firm.

To Freeze:
Cut into desired serving sizes or leave whole. Cover securely with foil and freeze for up to 2 months.

Make Mine Mocha!
If you want a "very mocha-ish" pie, use coffee flavored ice cream in place of the chocolate ice cream.

To Serve:
Let stand 30 minutes. Top with crumbled Heath bar.

Blueberry Delight

6-9 servings

1 (21 ounce) can blueberry pie filling
1 (12 ounce) can evaporated milk
¼ cup lemon juice
½ teaspoon almond extract
8 ounces whipped topping

For serving day:
berry sauce (optional, see page XX)
additional whipped topping

Combine first four ingredients in a bowl. Fold in whipped topping to blend well. Spread into an 11 x 7 x 2-inch dish and freeze until set.

To Freeze:
Cover with foil and freeze for up to 2 months.

To Serve:
Remove from freezer 20 minutes before serving. Cut into squares and top with additional whipped topping and berry sauce, if desired.

Darlene's 5 Minute Fudge

64 candies

⅔ cup Carnation milk
1⅔ cups sugar
½ teaspoon salt
1½ cups miniature marshmallows
1½ cups semisweet chocolate chips
1 teaspoon vanilla

Over medium heat bring milk, sugar and salt to a boil. Cook 5 minutes, stirring constantly. Remove from heat. Add in miniature marshmallows, chocolate chips and vanilla. Stir until marshmallows melt and fudge is smooth, about 1 minute. Pour into buttered 8-inch square pan. Cool. Cut into1-inch squares.

To Freeze:
Store squares between layers of waxed paper in an airtight container. Keeps for 1 month.

CHAPTER NINE

The Plans

The Art of the Mini-Session

I've discovered as people become more experienced and adept at cooking for the freezer, they often switch from doing a full, one-day-each-month cooking-frenzy to using a simpler process referred to as the "mini-session" in this book. A mini-session consists of choosing one main ingredient, such as chicken, and then preparing a group of chicken recipes in a single afternoon or evening. A mini-session usually involves only an hour or two of cooking, rather than the eight to ten hours often required for a complete month of cooking.

By watching for main ingredients to go on sale at your local market, you can stock up on large quantities and take advantage of great prices. For example, if you stock up on lean ground beef at this week's sale, a relatively short mini-session could easily supply you with five to ten ground beef meals to tuck away in the freezer. When chicken goes on sale later in the month, you can add another five to ten meals to your personal stash of "Frozen Assets". Simply by purchasing and cooking in bulk as you follow the sale flyers from the grocery store, you can save a great deal of time and money without ever investing an entire day in a monthly cooking session.

My book, *Frozen Assets Lite and Easy*, focuses on the mini-session method; but that doesn't mean it can't be flexible and easily adaptable for those readers who prefer the one-day-a-month procedure. If you want to do a full month of cooking in one day, simply double or triple several mini-sessions and then prepare these sessions together in one day. A full day of cooking for the freezer is essentially just a series of mini-sessions. Most cooks will prepare all their ground meat recipes together, then the chicken recipes, then spaghetti sauce based recipes, then vegetarian or bean recipes.

The great thing about breaking this all down into mini-sessions is that it allows you to build a month's worth of recipes around your family's specific tastes. Instead of trying to pull apart a 30-Day Meal Plan and change one disliked recipe, you can build your menus around mini-sessions that the family enjoys. Many people also find it easier to build their own mini-sessions to incorporate into their own "Frozen Assets" regimen. Be flexible. Take your favorite recipes from *Frozen Assets One* and build them into a mini-session. Build your own mini-sessions. Use the mini-sessions offered in this book. Combine all three ideas. Whatever you choose—a boundless array of easy-meal choices awaits you!

Mini-Session Menu # 1

Old-fashioned Chicken and Rice ~74
Chicken Vegetable Skillet ~ 84
Chicken Pasta Italiano ~ 85
Chicken Noodle Soup ~ 45
Mushroom Chicken Couscous ~ 54

Shopping List

MEAT
- ☐ 6 pounds boneless, skinless chicken breasts

DAIRY
- ☐ Margarine
- ☐ Parmesan cheese
- ☐ 2 cups skim milk

BREAD / PASTA
- ☐ 1½ cups long grain white rice
- ☐ 6 ounces bow tie pasta
- ☐ 5 ounces wide egg noodles
- ☐ 1½ cups couscous

VEGETABLES
- ☐ 6 large onions
- ☐ 1 bunch fresh parsley
- ☐ 14 garlic cloves
- ☐ 1 small green bell pepper
- ☐ 2 small red bell peppers
- ☐ 1 bunch fresh cilantro
- ☐ 4 large carrots
- ☐ 1 large celery rib
- ☐ 1 pound potatoes
- ☐ 3 medium tomatoes
- ☐ 2 small zucchini
- ☐ 12 ounces mushrooms, sliced

CANNED / BOXED
- ☐ 92 ounces (11½ cups) canned fat-free chicken broth
- ☐ 1 (6 ounce) jar sliced mushrooms
- ☐ 1 (16 ounce) can Italian-style stewed tomatoes

SPICES

- ☐ poultry seasonings
- ☐ thyme
- ☐ salt
- ☐ pepper
- ☐ Italian seasoning
- ☐ cayenne

FROZEN

- ☐ ½ cup frozen peas

MISCELLANEOUS

- ☐ olive oil
- ☐ vegetable oil
- ☐ cooking spray
- ☐ cooking sherry
- ☐ soy sauce
- ☐ cornstarch
- ☐ white vinegar

Mini-Session Menu # 2

Country Beef Soup ~ 46
Old-Fashioned Beef Stew ~ 94
Braised Beef ~ 76
Beef Fajitas ~ 77
Beef and Noodle ~79

Shopping List

MEAT
- [ ] 6 pounds lean boneless beef

DAIRY
- [ ] 8 ounces reduced-fat Cheddar cheese
- [ ] margarine
- [ ] fat-free sour cream

BREAD / PASTA
- [ ] 12 flour tortillas
- [ ] 6 ounces wide egg noodles

VEGETABLES
- [ ] 10 medium onions
- [ ] 1 pound potatoes
- [ ] 1 pound small red potatoes
- [ ] 3 large ribs celery
- [ ] 1 green bell pepper
- [ ] 1½ cups baby carrots
- [ ] 4½ cups mushrooms
- [ ] 1½ pounds carrots
- [ ] 3 garlic cloves
- [ ] 1½ cups pearl onions
- [ ] 1 head lettuce

CANNED / BOXED
- [ ] 2 cans Italian-style stewed tomatoes
- [ ] 36 ounces (4½ cups) canned fat-free beef broth
- [ ] 6 packets instant beef broth and seasoning mix
- [ ] small can tomato paste

SPICES
- [ ] parsley
- [ ] salt

- ❏ pepper
- ❏ flour
- ❏ thyme
- ❏ tarragon
- ❏ bay leaves
- ❏ oregano
- ❏ cumin
- ❏ paprika

FROZEN
- ❏ 1 cup frozen whole kernel corn

MISCELLANEOUS
- ❏ olive oil
- ❏ dry red wine
- ❏ lime juice
- ❏ 1 cup salsa
- ❏ prepared mustard
- ❏ red-wine vinegar

Mini-Session Menu # 3

Vegetable Fried Rice ~ 101
Ricotta Broccoli Pie ~ 102
Cheese and Veggie Quesadillas ~103
Three Cheese Lasagna ~104

Shopping List

DAIRY
- ☐ 4 cups skim milk
- ☐ 7 eggs
- ☐ 2 ounces Gruyere cheese
- ☐ 2 ounces reduced-fat mozzarella cheese
- ☐ 4 ounces reduced-fat Monterey Jack cheese
- ☐ 1 cup reduced-fat ricotta cheese
- ☐ 1 small container fat-free sour cream
- ☐ Parmesan cheese
- ☐ margarine

BREAD / PASTA
- ☐ 1 pound green-spinach lasagna noodles
- ☐ 12 flour tortillas
- ☐ long grain rice

VEGETABLES
- ☐ 1 large red bell pepper
- ☐ 1 bunch green onions
- ☐ 1 large leek
- ☐ 1 pound carrots
- ☐ 1 orange (for zest)
- ☐ 9 garlic cloves
- ☐ 1 small bunch fresh cilantro
- ☐ 1 fresh ginger root

CANNED / BOXED
- ☐ 6 ounces canned black beans
- ☐ 4 ounces canned green chilies
- ☐ 1 cup salsa

SPICES
- ☐ basil
- ☐ nutmeg
- ☐ salt

- [ ] pepper
- [ ] sugar
- [ ] flour

FROZEN
- [ ] 2 (10 ounce) packages frozen broccoli pieces

MISCELLANEOUS
- [ ] lime juice
- [ ] cider vinegar
- [ ] olive oil
- [ ] soy sauce
- [ ] oriental sesame oil
- [ ] ½ cup unsalted peanuts

Mini-Session Menu # 4

Turkey Roll-Ups ~ 75
Turkey Tetrazzini ~ 69
Turkey Green-Chile Soup ~49
Turkey & Asparagus Strata ~ 72
Spaghetti Pie ~ 109

Shopping List

DAIRY
- ☐ Margarine
- ☐ ½ cup parmesan cheese
- ☐ 6 eggs
- ☐ 1 cup fat-free cottage cheese
- ☐ 8 ounces reduce-fat Cheddar cheese
- ☐ 3 cups skim milk
- ☐ ¼ cup parmesan cheese

MEAT
- ☐ 12 ounces lean ground turkey
- ☐ 1 pound turkey (to cut into cubes)
- ☐ 8 thick slices of deli turkey-breast meat

BREAD & PASTA
- ☐ 10 slices of white bread
- ☐ 16 ounces spaghetti noodles

VEGETABLES
- ☐ 2 large leeks
- ☐ 2 large celery ribs
- ☐ 9 baby carrots
- ☐ 1 cup green chilies
- ☐ 3 onions
- ☐ 4 garlic cloves
- ☐ 5 asparagus stocks (or enough to equal one cup)
- ☐ 3 cups sliced mushrooms

CANNED / BOXED
- ☐ 9 cups chicken stock
- ☐ 1 cup evaporated skim milk
- ☐ 1 (16 ounce) can italian-style stewed tomatoes
- ☐ 1 (6 ounce) can tomato paste
- ☐ 1 box stove-top® stuffing mix
- ☐ 1 jar fat-free turkey gravy

SPICES / BAKING
- [ ] salt and pepper
- [ ] oregano
- [ ] sugar
- [ ] flour
- [ ] thyme
- [ ] parsley

MISC.
- [ ] olive oil
- [ ] vegetable oil
- [ ] 1 teaspoon Dijon mustard
- [ ] ½ cup dry white wine

CHAPTER TEN

Worksheets

Weekly Planner

MONDAY
TUESDAY
WEDNESDAY
THURSDAY
FRIDAY
SATURDAY
SUNDAY

Freezer Labels

Make photocopies of these labels and store them in a container with tape and a permanent marker. This will give you quick access to a reminder label for your meals.

Recipe Name: Number of Servings: Date Frozen: Reheating Instructions: Needed for serving day:	Recipe Name: Number of Servings: Date Frozen: Reheating Instructions: Needed for serving day:
Recipe Name: Number of Servings: Date Frozen: Reheating Instructions: Needed for serving day:	Recipe Name: Number of Servings: Date Frozen: Reheating Instructions: Needed for serving day:

Household Master Shopping List

VEGETABLES
__Asparagus
__Avocados
__Beens
__Beets
__Broccoli
__Cabbage
__Carrots
__Cauliflower
__Celery
__Corn
__Cucumber
__Garlic
__Ginger
__Lettuce
__Mushrooms
__Onions
__Peas
__Peppers
__Potatoes
__Radishes
__Spinach
__Squash
__Tomatoes
_____
_____
_____
_____
_____
_____

MEAT & FISH
__Bacon
__Beef
__Chicken
__Cold Cuts
__Fish
__Frankfurters
__Ham
__Hamburger
__Lamb
__Liver

__Oysters
__Pork
__Roast
__Salmon
__Saradines
__Sausage
__Shrimp
__Spare Ribs
__Steak
__Turkey
__Tuna
__Veal
_____
_____
_____
_____

FRUITS
__Apples
__Apricots
__Bananas
__Berries
__Cantaloupe
__Cherries
__Grapefruit
__Grapes
__ Honeydew
__Lemons
__Limes
__Oranges
__Peaches
__Pears
__Pineapple
__Prunes
__Raisins
__Strawberries
__Tangerines
__Watermelon
_____
_____
_____
_____

STAPLES & PANTRY
__Gelatin
__Honey
__Jam - Jelly
__Ketchup
__Macaroni
__Mayonnaise
__Mustard
__Milk - Canned
__Noodles
__Olives
__Oil - Cooking
__Pancake Mix
__Peanut Butter
__Pepper
__Pickles
__Potato Chips
__Pretzels
__Pudding
__Rice
__Salad Oil
__Salt
__Shortening
__Soups
__Spaghetti
__Spices
__Sugar
__Syrup
__Tortilla Chips
__Vinegar
__Baby Food
__king Powder
__Bar B-Q Sauce
__Cake Mix
__Candy
__Cereal
__Chili
__Chocolate
__Extract
__Flour

BREADS
__Biscuits
__Bread
__Cakes
__Cookies
__Crackers
__Donuts
__Pies
__Rolls

_____
_____
_____

BEVERAGES
__Cocoa Mix
__Coffee
__Fruit Juices
__Juice Boxes
__Kool-Aid
__Soft Drinks
__Tea

_____
_____
_____

DAIRY
__Butter
__Cheese
__Cottage
  Cheese
__Cream
__ Cream
  Cheese
__Eggs
__Ice Cream
__Margarine
__Milk
__Whipped
  Cream
__ Yogurt

_____
_____
_____

MISC.
__Aluminum Foil
__Cleanser
__Dish Soap
__Film
__ Foil Pans
__ Freezer Bags
__Hand Soap
__ Lunch Bags
__Matches
__Napkins
__Paper Plates
__Paper Towels
__Pet Food
__ Permanent
  Marker
__Polish
__Plastic Cups
__Plastic Wrap
__Scouring Pads
__Sponges
__Tissue -
  Bathroom
__Tissue - Facial
__Tooth Paste
__Waxed Paper
__Air Freshener
__Batteries
__Broom
__Carpet
  Freshener
__Light Bulbs

_____
_____

LAUNDRY & HEALTH
__ Band-Aids
__Bleach
__Coat Hangers
__Clothespins
__Detergent
__Dryer Sheets
__Fabric Softener
__Spot Remover
__Starch
__Aspirin
__ Ibuprofen
__Cold Medicines
__Diapers
__Toothbrush
__Toothpaste
__Wet-Wipes
__Body Lotion
__Conditioner
__Cologne
__Cosmetics
__Deodorant
__Hair Spray
__Hairbrush
__Nail Care
__ Raszer
__Shampoo
__ Shaving
  Cream
__Soap

_____
_____
_____

Master Freezer Inventory

Meal Name & Date Frozen	Number of Meals in Freezer									
	1	2	3	4	5	6	7	8	9	10

HOW TO USE YOUR FREEZER INVENTORY:
Make copies of this freezer inventory and post one on your freezer. Record each meal you prepare along with the date it was frozen. Place a slash mark across the number of meals you have prepared—i.e. if you prepared 6 meals, place a slash mark in the boxes labeled 1-6. As you use each meal, turn the slash mark into an X to indicate it was used.

Weights and Measures

A dash = less than 1/8 teaspoon
4 tablespoons = 1/4 cup
1/2 cup = 8 tablespoons teaspoons
1/2 pint = 1 cup
4 quarts = 1 gallon
8 ounces = 1/2 pound
16 ounces = 1 pound
64 ounces = 1/2 gallon
1 quart = .95 liter

3 teaspoons = 1 tablespoon
1/3 cup = 5 tablespoons + 1 teaspoon
2/3 cup = 10 tablespoons + 2
1 quart = 4 cups
8 ounces = 1 cup liquid
16 ounces = 2 pints or ½ quart liquid
32 ounces = 1 quart
1 liter = 1.06 quarts

Equivalents: US=Australia/UK

1/8 teaspoon=0.5 ml
1/2 teaspoon=2 ml
1 tablespoon=1 tablespoon
1/3 cup=1/4 cup=3 fluid ounces=90 ml
2/3 cup=1/2 cup=5 fluid ounces=150 ml
1 cup=3/4 cup=8 fluid ounces=240 ml
2 cups=1 pint
1 ounce=30 grams
1/4 pound=125 grams
1 pound=500 grams=1/2 kilogram

1/4 teaspoon=1 ml
1 teaspoon=5 ml
1/4 cup=2 tablespoons=2 fluid ounces=60 ml
1/2 cup=1/3 cup=4 fluid ounces=120 ml
3/4 cup=2/3 cup=6 fluid ounces=180 ml
1 cup
1 quart=1 liter
2 ounces=60 grams
1/2 pound=225 grams

Temperature
Fahrenheit/Celsius (in degrees)

32	0
212	100
250	120
275	140
300	150
325	160
350	180
375	190
400	200
425	220
450	230
475	240
500	260

Baking Pan Sizes

American	Metric
8x1 ½-inch round	20x4cm cake tin
9x1 ½-inch round	23x3.5cm cake tin
11x7x1 ½ inch baking pan	28x18x4cm baking tin
13x9x2-inch baking pan	30x20x3cm baking tin
2 quart rectangular dish	30x20x3cm baking tin
15x10x2-inch baking pan	30x25x2cm baking tin
9-inch pie plate	22x4 or 23x4cm pie plate
7 or 8-inch springform pan	9x5x3-inch loaf pan
1 ½ quart casserole	1.5 liter casserole
2 quart casserole	2 liter casserole

Yields and Equivalents

Apple	1 medium, chopped=about 1 cup
	3 medium=1 pound or 2 and 3/4 cups, sliced
Bacon	½ cup crumbled=8 slices crisply cooked
Bananas	3 large or 4 small=2 cups sliced or 1 1/3 cups mashed
Beans, dried	1 cup =2and 1/4 to 2 and 1/2 cups cooked
Beef, cooked	1 cup 1/2 inch pieces=5 ounces
Butter	1 ounce butter=2 tablespoons
	1 stick butter=1/4 pound or 8 ounces
	1 cup butter=2 sticks or 1/2 pound
Celery	2 medium stalks=2/3 to 3/4 cup
Cheese	1 pound=4 cups shredded
	1 cup shredded=1/4 pound
	2 cups cottage cheese=16 ounces
	6 tablespoons cream cheese=3 ounces
Cherries	1/2 pound=1 cup pitted
Chocolate	1 ounce=1 square
	1 cup chips=6 ounces
Cranberries	1 cup fresh makes 1 cup sauce
	1 pound=4 cups
Crumbs	1 cup cracker crumbs=28 saltine crackers
	1 cup graham cracker crumbs=14 square graham crackers
	1 cup cracker crumbs=24 rich round crackers
	1 cup bread crumbs=soft 1 and 1/2 slices or dry 4 slices
	1 cup vanilla wafer crumbs=22 wafers
	1 cup chocolate wafer crumbs=19 wafers
Eggs	1 cup=4 large eggs
	1/2 cup liquid egg subsitute=1 egg
	1 cup egg yolks=10 to 12 egg yolks
	1 cup egg whites=8 to 10 egg whites

Garlic powder	1 clove fresh=1/2 teaspoon chopped or 1/8 teaspoon garlic
Grapes	1 pound=2 cups halved
Green Pepper	1 large=1 cup diced
Herbs	1 tablespoon fresh, snipped=1 teaspoon dried or ½ teaspoon ground
Lemon	Juice of 1 lemon=3 tablespoons
	grated peel of 1 lemon=about 1 teaspoon
Lettuce	6 cups bite-size pieces=1-pound head
Macaroni	1 to 1 and 1/4 cups=4 ounces or 2 to 2 and 1/2 cups cooked
	16 ounces=about 8 cups cooked
Marshmallows	10 minature=1 large
	1 cup=11 large
Mushrooms	8 ounces= 2 and 1/2 cups sliced or 1 cup cooked
(Fresh)	1 cup sliced and cooked=4 ounce can, drained
Mustard	1 teaspoon dry=1 tablespoon prepared
Nuts	1 cup chopped=1/4 pound or 4 ounces
	1 cup whole or halved= 4 to 5 ounces
Oats	1 and 3/4 cups cooked=1 cup raw
Olives	24 small=2 ounces=about ½ cup sliced
Onions	1 medium, chopped= ½ cup
	1 medium=1 teaspoon onion powder or 1 tablespoon dried minced
Orange	Juice of one orange=1/3 to 1/2 cup
	Grated peel of 1 orange=2 tablespoons
Peaches/Pears	1 medium=1/2 cup sliced
Potatoes	3 medium=2 cups sliced or cubed
	3 medium=1 and 3/4 mashed
Rice	1 cup white rice(long grain)=about 7 ounces=3 to 4 cups cooked
	1 cup white rice(instant)=2 cups cooked
	1 cup brown rice=3 cups cooked
	1 cup wild rice=3 to 4 cups cooked
	1 pound cooked wild rie=2 2/3 cup dry
Sour cream	1 cup=8 ounces
Spaghetti and Noodles	
	8 ounces=4 cups cooked
	1 pound=8 cups cooked
Strawberries	1 quart=2 cups sliced
Sugar	Powdered / 4 cups=1 pound
	Brown / 2 and 1/4 cups, packed=1 pound
	Granulated / 2 cups=1 pound
Tomatoes	1 cup canned=1 1/3 cups fresh, cut up
Whipping Cream	1 cup=2 cups whipped
Yeast	1 package=2 and 1/4 teaspoons regular or quick active dry

Emergency Substitutions

Baking Powder:	1 teaspoon=1/2 teaspoon cream of tartar plus 1/4 teaspoon baking soda
Balsamic Vinegar:	Sherry or cider vinegar
Beer:	Apple juice or beef broth
Broth:	1 teaspoon granulated or 1 cube bouillon dissolved in one cup water
Brown Sugar, Packed:	Equal amount of granulated sugar
Buttermilk:	1 teaspoon lemon juice or vinegar plus milk to make 1 cup; let stand 5 minutes
Cajun Seasoning:	Equal parts white pepper, black pepper, ground red pepper, onion powder, garlic powder and paprika
Chocolate:	1 square, unsweetened:3 tablespoons cocoa plus 1 tablespoon butter. For 1 square semisweet: 1 square unsweetened+1 tablespoon sugar For 2 squares, semisweet: 1/3 cup semisweet chips
Corn Syrup:	For light or dark: 1 cup + 1/4 cup water For dark:1 cup light corn syrup or 1 cup maple syrup or 3/4 light corn syrup + 1/4 cup molasses
Cornstarch:	For 1 tablespoon: 2 tablespoons all-purpose flour
Cream of Mushroom Soup:	For one can: 1 cup thick white sauce + 4 ounce can mushrooms, drained and chopped
Eggs:	For 1 egg: 2 egg whites or 2 egg yolks or 1/4 cup liquid egg substitute
Flour: Cake flour: Self-rising:	1 cup minus 2 tablespoons all-purpose flour. 1 cup all-purpose flour + 1 teaspoon baking powder and 1/2 teaspoon salt.
Honey:	1 and 1/4 cup sugar +1/4 cup water
Leeks:	Equal amounts green onions or shallots
Lemon Juice:	For 1 teaspoon: 1 teaspoon cider vinegar or white vinegar
Milk:	½ cup evaporated(not condensed) milk plus 1/2 cup water
Molasses:	Equal amount honey
Mushrooms:	For 1 cup cooked: 4 ounce can, drained
Poultry Seasoning:	For 1 teaspoon: 3/4 teaspoon sage + 1/4 teaspoon thyme
Pumpkin Pie Spice:	For 1 teaspoon:1/2 teaspoon cinnamon + 1/4 teaspoon ground ginger + 1/8 teaspoon ground allspice + 1/8 teaspoon ground nutmeg
Red Pepper Sauce:	4 drops=1/8 teaspoon ground cayenne(red) pepper

Sour Cream:	equal amount of plain yogurt
Tomato sauce:	For 2 cups sauce: 3/4 cups paste + 1and 1/4 cup water
Wine: For white:	apple juice, apple cider, white grape juice, chicken or
vegetable	
	broth, water.
For red:	apple cider, chicken, beef or vegetable broth, water.
Yogurt:	equal amounts of sour cream

Freezer Storage

Breads, Baked	2 to 3 months
Cakes	3 to 4 months
Cookies	3 to 4 months
Dairy Products:	
Butter or Margarine	9 to 12 months
Cottage Cheese	3 months
Cream	1 to 4 months
Hard Natural Cheese	6 months
Processed Cheese	6 months
Soft cheese	6 months
Yogurt	1 to 2 months
Eggs:	
Whole eggs	Do not freeze
Egg yolks (cover in water)	1 year
Egg whites	1 year
Egg substitute	1 year
Fruits/Juices	8 to 12 months
Meats:	
Beef, roasts or steaks	6 to 12 months
Beef, ground	3 months
Beef, stew meat	3 to 6 months
Lamb	6 to 9 months
Pork, roast or chops	3 to 6 months
Pork, ground	2 months
Veal	6 to 9 months
Cured meat, ham or bacon	1 to 2 months
Hot dogs	1 to 2 months
Sausages	2 to 3 months
Poultry, pieces	6 months
Poultry, whole	1 year
Fish-fatty(salmon,mackerel, trout)	2 months

Fish-lean(cod,haddock,pike)	6 months
Fish-breaded,cooked	2 to 3 months
Shellfish	2 to 4 months
Pies, Baked or Pie shells	4 months
Pies, unbaked	2 months
Nuts, shelled	3 months
Vegetables	8 months

Cooked Foods:

Casseroles	3 months
Meat	1 to 3 months
Soups	4 months

Refrigerator Storage

(Always check dates on package before purchasing)

Breads	5 to 7 days
Condiments	12 months

Dairy:

Buttermilk	2 weeks
Sour cream	2 weeks
Yogurt	2 weeks
Cottage Cheese	10 to 30 days
Cream Cheese	2 weeks
Hard Cheese	3 to 4 weeks
Sliced Cheese	2 weeks
Spread Cheese	1 to 2 weeks
Cream, heavy	3 to 5 days
Cream, half-and-half	3 to 5 days
Milk	5 days

Eggs, whole	1 week
Eggs, yolks or whites	2 to 4 days

Butter	2 weeks
Margarine	1 month
Mayonnaise	6 months
Salad Dressings	6 months

Fruit:

Apples	1 month
Apricots	3 to 5 days
Avocados	3 to 5 days
Berries	2 to 3 days

Cranberries	1 week
Citrus	2 weeks
Dried fruits	6 months
Grapes	3 to 5 days
Melons	3 to 5 days
Peaches	3 to 5 days
Pears	3 to 5 days
Pineapple	2 to 3 days
Plums	3 to 5 days

Meat, Poultry, Seafood:
Fresh:

Chops	3 to 5 days
Ground	1 to 2 days
Roasts	3 to 5 days
Steaks	3 to 5 days

Processed:

Cold cuts(unopened)	2 weeks
Cold cuts(opened)	3 to 5 days
Cured bacon	1 week
Hot dogs	1 week
Ham-sliced	3 to 5 days
Ham-whole	1 week
Poultry/Seafood	1 to 2 days

Vegetables:

Asparagus	2 to 3 days
Broccoli	3 to 5 days
Cabbage	2 weeks
Carrots	2 weeks
Cauliflower	1 week
Celery	1 week
Corn, sweet	1 day
Cucumbers	1 week
Green Beans	1 week
Green Onions	3 to 5 days
Green Peas	3 to 5 days
Green Peppers	1 weeks
Lettuce	3 to 5 days
Radishes	2 weeks
Tomatoes	1 week
Squash	3 to 5 days

CHAPTER ELEVEN

Your Recipes

Use this section to record your own Frozen Favorites! Photocopy these pages to provide a central storage solution for your favorite recipes.

Recipe Name: _____
Servings: _____

Ingredients:
_____
_____
_____
_____
_____
_____
_____
_____
_____
_____

Preparation Instructions:
_____
_____
_____
_____
_____

Freezing Instructions:
_____
_____
_____
_____

Thawing & Reheating Instructions:
_____
_____
_____
_____
_____
_____

Notes:

Recipe Name: _____

Servings: _____

Ingredients:

_____

_____

_____

_____

_____

_____

_____

_____

_____

_____

_____

_____

Preparation Instructions:

_____

_____

_____

_____

_____

Freezing Instructions:

_____

_____

_____

_____

_____

Thawing & Reheating Instructions:

_____

_____

_____

_____

_____

_____

Notes:

Recipe Name: _____

Servings:

Ingredients:

_____

_____

_____

_____

_____

_____

_____

_____

_____

_____

Preparation Instructions:

_____

_____

_____

_____

Freezing Instructions:

_____

_____

_____

_____

Thawing & Reheating Instructions:

_____

_____

_____

_____

_____

_____

Notes:

Recipe Name: _____

Servings: _____

Ingredients:

_____

_____

_____

_____

_____

_____

_____

_____

_____

_____

Notes:

Preparation Instructions:

_____

_____

_____

_____

_____

Freezing Instructions:

_____

_____

_____

_____

Thawing & Reheating Instructions:

_____

_____

_____

_____

_____

_____

_____

Recipe Name:

Servings:

Ingredients:

_____

_____

_____

_____

_____

_____

_____

_____

_____

_____

_____

Preparation Instructions:

_____

_____

_____

_____

_____

Freezing Instructions:

_____

_____

_____

_____

_____

Thawing & Reheating Instructions:

_____

_____

_____

_____

_____

_____

Notes:

Recipe Name: _____

Servings: _____

Ingredients:

_____
_____
_____
_____
_____
_____
_____
_____
_____
_____

Notes:

Preparation Instructions:

_____
_____
_____
_____
_____

Freezing Instructions:

_____
_____
_____
_____
_____

Thawing & Reheating Instructions:

_____
_____
_____
_____
_____
_____
_____
_____

Recipe Name:

Servings:

Ingredients:

_____

_____

_____

_____

_____

_____

_____

_____

_____

Preparation Instructions:

_____

_____

_____

_____

Freezing Instructions:

_____

_____

_____

_____

Thawing & Reheating Instructions:

_____

_____

_____

_____

_____

_____

_____

Notes:

Recipe Name: _____

Servings: _____

Ingredients:

_____

_____

_____

_____

_____

_____

_____

_____

_____

_____

_____

Preparation Instructions:

_____

_____

_____

_____

_____

Freezing Instructions:

_____

_____

_____

_____

Thawing & Reheating Instructions:

_____

_____

_____

_____

_____

_____

Notes:

Recipe Name:
Servings:

Ingredients:

_____
_____
_____
_____
_____
_____
_____
_____
_____
_____
_____

Preparation Instructions:

_____
_____
_____
_____
_____

Freezing Instructions:

_____
_____
_____
_____
_____

Thawing & Reheating Instructions:

_____
_____
_____
_____
_____
_____
_____

Notes:

Recipe Name:

Servings:

Ingredients:

_____

_____

_____

_____

_____

_____

_____

_____

_____

_____

_____

Preparation Instructions:

_____

_____

_____

_____

_____

Freezing Instructions:

_____

_____

_____

_____

_____

Thawing & Reheating Instructions:

_____

_____

_____

_____

_____

_____

_____

Notes:

Recipe Name: _____

Servings:

Ingredients:
_____
_____
_____
_____
_____
_____
_____
_____
_____
_____

Preparation Instructions:
_____
_____
_____
_____
_____

Freezing Instructions:
_____
_____
_____
_____
_____

Thawing & Reheating Instructions:
_____
_____
_____
_____
_____
_____
_____

Notes:

Recipe Name:

Servings:

Ingredients:

_____
_____
_____
_____
_____
_____
_____
_____
_____
_____

Preparation Instructions:

_____
_____
_____
_____
_____

Freezing Instructions:

_____
_____
_____
_____

Thawing & Reheating Instructions:

_____
_____
_____
_____
_____
_____
_____

Notes:

Recipe Name:

Servings:

Ingredients:

_____
_____
_____
_____
_____
_____
_____
_____
_____
_____

Preparation Instructions:

_____
_____
_____
_____
_____

Freezing Instructions:

_____
_____
_____
_____
_____

Thawing & Reheating Instructions:

_____
_____
_____
_____
_____
_____
_____
_____

Notes:

Recipe Name: _____

Servings: _____

Ingredients:

_____

_____

_____

_____

_____

_____

_____

_____

_____

_____

_____

Preparation Instructions:

_____

_____

_____

_____

_____

Freezing Instructions:

_____

_____

_____

_____

_____

Thawing & Reheating Instructions:

_____

_____

_____

_____

_____

_____

_____

Notes:

Checkout these online service brought to you by Champion Press, Ltd.

WWW.RUSHHOURCOOK.COM

Quick recipes.
Fun trivia.
Real advice.
Join the free "Daily Rush" cooking club.

THE FIVE RULES OF RUSH HOUR RECIPES:

1. All ingredients may be pronounced accurately through the phonetic use of the English Language.

2. Each ingredient can be located in the market without engaging on a full-scale scavenger hunt.

3. No list of ingredients shall be longer than the instructions.

4. Each recipe is durable enough to survive the Queen-of-Incapable Cooking and elicit a compliment.

5. The Rush Hour Cook's finicky child will eat it—or some portion of it.

www.womeninwellness.com

IT'S ALL ABOUT YOU!
fitness…with a twist

What's different about Women in Wellness?

*1. A whole-approach to wellness, covering physical, emotional and
spiritual health
2. Interactive one-on-one coaching and customized planning
3. Sister in Success support program
4. We give you points, redeemable for prizes as you reach your goals!*

change your life with a click…
visit us today for a free 30 day trial!

Also available from Champion Press, Ltd.

by Deborah Taylor-Hough
Frozen Assets: Cook for a Day, Eat for a Month $14.95
Frozen Assets Lite & Easy: Cook for a Day, Eat for a Month $14.95
Mix and Match Recipe: Creative Recipes for Busy Kitchens $9.95
A Simple Choice: a practical guide for saving your time, money and sanity $14.95

Other favorite cookbooks by Champion Press, Ltd.:
Cooking for Blondes: gourmet recipes for the culinarily challenged by Rhonda Levtich $27.95/hardcover $16/paperback

365 Quick, Easy and Inexpensive Dinner Menus by Penny E. Stone (Over 1000 recipes!)

The Frantic Family Cookbook: mostly healthy meals in minutes by Leanne Ely $29.95 hardcover, $14.95 paperback

Healthy Foods: an irreverent guide to understanding nutrition and feeding your family well by Leanne Ely $19.95

The Rush Hour Cook: Family Favorites by Brook Noel $5.95

The Rush Hour Cook: One-Pot Wonders by Brook Noel $5.95

The Rush Hour Cook: Effortless Entertaining by Brook Noel $5.95

The Rush Hour Cook: Presto Pasta by Brook Noel $5.95

The Rush Hour Cook:; Weekly Wonders $16

Crazy About Crockpots: 101 Easy & Inexpensive Recipes for Less than .75 cents a serving by Penny Stone

Crazy About Crockpots: 101 Soups & Stews for Less than .75 cents a serving by Penny Stone

Crazy About Crockpots: 101 Recipes for Entertaining at Less than .75 cents a serving by Penny Stone

TO ORDER
read excerpts, sample recipes, order books and more at
www.championpress.com

or send a check payable to Champion Press, Ltd. to 4308 Blueberry Road, Fredonia, WI 53021. Please include $3.95 shipping & handling for the first book and $1 for each additional book.